COYOTE SONGS

COYOTE SONGS

TALES FROM THE WESTERN ROAD

Ron W. Marr

Writers Club Press

San Jose New York Lincoln Shanghai

COYOTE SONGS
Tales From The Western Road

Writers Club Press
an imprint of iUniverse.com, Inc.

For information address:
iUniverse.com, Inc.
620 North 48th Street, Suite 201
Lincoln, NE 68504-3467
www.iuniverse.com

ISBN: 0-595-13119-0

Printed in the United States of America

This Book Is Dedicated To The Memory Of The Late David Thomas Hays, Author, Hermit & Fellow Founding Member Of The Literary Terrorists

Contents

Epigraph

"Bend and you will be whole.

Curl and you will be straight.

Keep empty and you will be filled.

Grow old and you will be revered.

Have little and you will gain.

Have much and you will be confused."

Lao Tzu...from the Tao Teh Ching

"If I want to be amused, I can see that I'm going to have to do it myself."

Ron Marr

Preface

Life is rarely well ordered, and in that sense the essays in this anthology follow suit. Most, with a few bare exceptions, were taken from the newspaper column I've syndicated for near a decade around the Rocky Mountains and the Dakotas. They are stories of old friends and loose ends, vignettes of love, existence and other fanciful notions. They are, perhaps, a peephole view into the inner sanctum of a Rocky Mountain Beach Bum, a meandering travelogue stretching from the Florida beaches to the Ozark hills to Montana's Tobacco Root Mountains.

In the following pages one will find tall tales and diatribes, sonnets and siren songs. Hopefully, the reader will come away with a few laughs, a few smiles, a few tears and a few thoughts. Hopefully, at the end of the day, the reader will hear a few wild geese and notice a certain itchiness of the feet.

So open at page one or page 101. It doesn't matter where, when, how or why. My only desire is that you enjoy.

A thousand people made this book possible and I am grateful to all. However, a bare handful deserve special praise. My utmost gratitude goes to my parents, Bill and Ruth Marr, who always urged this wandering son to follow his heart, no matter how obscure the direction or how foggy the dream. Also, my deepest thanks go to Edward T. Boys and Wendy Feintech, old and dear friends who have stayed constant and strong over the fast-flying years. Last but not least, I once again offer my undying love and eternal devotion to the pack known as Crow, Buffett, Henry, Wowie, BJ, Tiger and Skipper. May there always be bones to chew, shoes to tear, cats to chase and long, smiling nights in front of the fire.

Ron Marr
Pony, Montana
May 1st, 2000

Introduction

There is a gigantic concrete goose outside of Sumner, Missouri, a big Canadian honker that stands nearly four stories high not including spotlights. This might strike some folks as an odd item in which a town should take pride; most places like to put up cute little parks or maybe a statue or three of dead Civil War heroes. Then again, not all towns are Sumner, home to the country's largest annual goose blasting festival.

I'm sure the northern Missouri village is known for things other than whacking geese with double ought steel shot. If memory serves it seems somebody once told me it was the birthplace of either General Omar Bradley or Clarabelle the Clown, but maybe that was some other speck on the map. After awhile all the towns and all the roads seem to look a lot alike. Wander enough and even General Omar and Clarabelle look a lot alike.

The only reason I recall Sumner, aside from the four story concrete goose, is because I visited there one weekend with Cole Paulson and Quick Roberts. Cole was a biologist who had landed a temporary job with this or that state conservation agency and was spending a season banding geese. He claimed to enjoy this job because it let him feel like a Delta Force commando on a raiding mission. Raiding Canadian honkers rather than Shiite Moslems was a ball of fun, according to Cole, with the obvious advantage being that Canadian Honkers don't try and zipper your chest with an Uzi.

The primary mission of a goose commando, for those who've never felt the call to service, is to slink through the bushes with a surplus Army mortar and fire a weighted net over the top of the feeding goose flocks. After the net perimeters are secured, it is the duty of the commando to wade in and herd the flailing creatures into a pen and put copper love bracelets around their tiny little legs. Cole said this could get you hurt, a goose is a powerful creature when irritated and dressed up in cheap jewelry, but was much more fun than the alternative.

A real commando has to endure all sorts of rough training and verbal abuse from officers. The job requires years of practice and taking orders from your boss and the constant risk of becoming dead in a variety of unsavory manners. Cole found being a goose commando to be a much more pleasant choice than being a real commando, and the chest freezer which he kept chock full of goose breast lended great credence to his survival skills. It also meant that none of us would go hungry for the weekend.

Cole was a laid back fellow, taking one day at a time and happy as hell as long as he was either fishing, hunting or capturing geese with a mortar. Quick, however, was exactly the opposite. He liked to cast and blast as well as we did, but there was always a slightly unstable side to the man that made you wonder if he was going to pull a knife or attack a college linebacker or go climbing naked on top of a gigantic concrete goose.

That weekend in Sumner, I saw him engage in at least two of these activities. The guy he pulled the knife on was a 300 pound farmer deep in the throes of a Jack Daniel's haze, so maybe we should go ahead and give Quick credit for the hat trick.

Sumner has a limited night life when the goose festival isn't going on, which means it's pretty damn boring for 362 days of the year. The big party was months away when Quick and I pulled up to Cole's cabin, and as a person can only spend so many nights eating goose breast and blasting at beer cans before boredom sets in, Cole set his mind to alternative entertainment. Being the good host, he suggested a night on the town was in order. In search of culture, we decided to visit the Sumner Tavern and shoot a few games of eight ball.

Eight ball is the standard recreational pursuit in any rural American community, and a town that doesn't have at least one bar with a beat-up eight ball table could not rightly call itself a town. Without a pool table there is nothing to occupy your time while sneaking lustful looks at the one or two local girls who have teeth. Without a pool table it is next to impossible to formulate the strategy of approaching the occasional misplaced female tourist, also with teeth, who might be lost off the interstate. These things require time and forethought. Just sitting at the bar and trying to impress some gal with your talent for French inhaling Camel Lights might work after midnight and about twenty shots of rum, but it's not all that attractive under normal circumstances.

The Sumner Tavern had a dandy pool table, a 25 cent per game version with mostly straight cues and an expanse of green felt with only one tear in it. The stools at the bar were of red vinyl. A sheer film of old smoke coated the glasses behind the bar. You could get anything you wanted at the Sumner Tavern, as long as it was beer or whiskey. You could even have dinner there, as long as you didn't want real food. Half a dozen vinegar filled gallon jugs of pickled eggs sat on the counter next to a rusty can of venison jerky. For Sumner, this was living at its finest.

We pretty much had the place to ourselves the evening we dropped by. Doris, a long retired Vegas showgirl who functioned as manager, bartender, and pickled egg waitress, made small talk and flirted like a schoolgirl whenever we slid up for another pitcher. She liked young men, and as there were no other women for us to drool over, we liked the attention. A curdled up old rummy sat silently at the bar contemplating his boilermaker, and while he luckily didn't flirt, he did keep mostly to himself. The rummy seemed deep in his own memories, and I think he had a bad case of the spirit being willing but the flesh being too weak to cooperate. He slurped his drink and occasionally threw a leering glance towards Doris's 60 year old posterior. She didn't seem to mind, and as long as things didn't get disgusting, neither did we.

Old folks in a bar shouldn't get all romantic, for it forces those of us who are still young and stupid enough to think we're charming to contemplate our own mortality. Plus, watching people with dentures gum each other is enough to make you wonder about the joys of sex and could lead to a severe alcohol problem.

Things were just fine, a slow night in a slow town. Quick was being well-behaved because he'd only had a twelve pack. Cole and I were having a grand old time missing shots and telling lies. With the help of Mr. Adolph Coors we'd forgotten that you couldn't let Quick out of your sight for more than thirty seconds. That boy could always manage to create a pound of trouble out of an ounce of nothing.

"Gimme' that damn camera," we heard The Bear roar from the back table of the bar. "I don't want nobody rememberin' me."

Cole and I looked up from the half-finished eight ball game in time to see the flashbulb go off for the second time. Quick was back-pedaling slowly in our direction. He had managed to find the one other member of the community, besides the rummy, who had ventured to the intimate confines of the Tavern on a tired Monday evening. Unfortunately, it was a hulking brute of a farmer whose wife had just run away with both his neighbor and bird dog. Quick, being the sensitive and artistic sort, felt the immediate urge to snap a few candid shots of the depressed monster for his scrapbook.

"Watch the birdie," he said, flicking off another Kodak moment.

"I told you I don't want nobody rememberin' me. Now gimme' that damn camera," reiterated The Bear.

Maybe a bear doesn't ordinarily wear a pair of overalls and a feed cap. Maybe he doesn't, at least as a rule, have Budweiser spilling down his face and axle grease under his fingernails. This one did, take my word for it. Maybe Marlon Perkins missed a few species when he was out categorizing the Wild Kingdom. Whatever the case, it seemed a poor idea that Quick had woken this bear from hibernation.

As the flash went off again, The Bear broke into a lurching stumble, massive biceps popping his threadbare flannel shirt and outrageous gut knocking tables aside as if they were cardboard cut-outs.

"I'm takin' that camera," The Bear said. "I told you I don't want nobody rememberin' me."

Cole and I looked at each other and grimaced. We had both broken out in an unsightly burst of perspiration that would have seemed quite inappropriate in more refined settings. We knew all too well that Quick had an inordinately over-developed sense of the sanctity of personal property, at least in the sense that he felt his property was sacred and everyone else's was fairly much worthless. He'd also proven about fifty times in the past year that he didn't mind getting into a eye-gouging contest with a bulldozer. This knowledge did little to ease our minds that the disagreement over a photo opportunity would be resolved in an amicable manner.

What we didn't expect was that Quick would slide a skinners knife out of a boot sheath. This was a new wrinkle. He usually only carried a roll of quarters for bar fights.

The skinners knife hit the table with a clank, the shining blade grinning against the green felt.

"Come and get it son," Quick growled, now sounding a bit like a wounded grizzly himself. "It's waitin' for you."

Cole and I looked at each other again. We both still had our pool cues and were desperately trying to decide whether it would be more effective to brain Quick or The Bear. We had almost reached a consensus that Quick was the easier target when the Rummy spoke for the first time of the night.

"He's gonna' shove that knife up your butt boy," the toothless old face cackled from the bar, "and it ain't a gonna' be the first time he done it to some hippy punk."

The term "hippy punk" probably hadn't been used anywhere but Sumner in fifteen years, but old traditions hold their value well in the Midwest. The message seemed the same no matter the vernacular. Somebody was in it up to their necks and that somebody most likely was us.

The Bear charged. Quick dropped into his favorite fighting stance, the one that usually ended up with somebody else's eyeballs rolling around on the floor. He had grown up on a notoriously vicious military base in the Ozarks, his father had been a gunboat pilot in Vietnam. The last thing Quick was known for was a clean fight ala the Marquess of Queensbury. We assumed, from past experience, that he had been taught just about every trick in the book and might have invented a couple of dozen himself.

A mere six feet separated the two when a baseball bat smashed into the bar and sent both Cole and I into something resembling cardiac arrest. Doris had spoken.

"I told you I didn't want no more trouble," she said to The Bear, shoving the Louisville Slugger under his chin. "If you'd treated your wife good she wouldn't have left. If you'd fed your dog she might have stayed. Now get the hell out of here and leave these boys alone."

In a remarkably insightful move, one that forever earned my gratitude because it allowed me to appear both mentally retarded and relatively innocent, Cole had pocketed the skinning knife and managed to back Quick into a convenient booth. I let out a deep breath, leaned against the bar, and thanked the Gods that all my teeth were still in my head and no local police were busting through the door. I looked at Doris and silently promised myself that I would always, for the rest of my life, flirt with older women. I also promised I would never take pictures of giant ugly people in small town taverns. Those who forget history are forever condemned to repeat it. I read that once, and time has proven it to be a truism. Especially in regards to unruly drunks who are bigger than me.

I watched The Bear slink out the door, head bowed and tail between his legs. Doris twirled the bat and offered me another beer. Quick simply sat staring at his camera with a smile on his face that could have lit up Times Square during a blackout. Simple pleasures meant a lot to him. After all, he only wanted a few souvenir photos of the single place in America with a four story, concrete Canadian goose with spotlights.

"I'm really sorry Doris," Cole said as he walked slowly to the bar, pulled out his wallet and offered to buy her a drink. "He just gets out of control sometimes."

"Don't you worry your head about it. That ol' boy has been in here for three nights runnin', blubberin' about his damn wife and his damn dog," she replied. "It was just a matter of time and I was sick of him anyway."

That was almost twenty years ago. I guess in some ways a lot has changed. In others it's just about the same. Sometimes you chase the wild goose on purpose, see it soaring through the air with the cry of freedom in its lungs. Other times it's just a big hunk of concrete, sitting there waiting for you to make a damn fool of yourself. I've seen and heard both. The problem with wild geese is that you never know which type you're chasing until the silly thing lands and you can get a good look at it.

And maybe that's what makes the whole party so much fun. The not knowing.

Since visiting the Sumner Tavern I've logged years of road time. It seems that the wild goose was always just overhead, flapping his wings toward tomorrow and honking his fool brains out. In the past, whenever I heard that plaintive wail my feet felt the itch and told me it was time to move on. When the wild goose honks, it is a veritable Siren Song. The urge to follow becomes impossible to refuse.

The journey has always seemed much more fun than the destination. The miles and smiles much more gratifying than the day to day grind. I'm not exactly sure why that is, but the idea of settling down for an extended period of time has usually stuck me as a death sentence. My married friends say this attitude is selfish, say that I will never grow up. They berate me for missing the joys of security and family. They could be right, but I don't think so. They just heard a different goose than I did. Individual choices are rarely either of the better or worse variety. They're just different, that's all.

While many of my landing strips have initially seemed the prettiest, or coolest or wildest spot on earth, after a short time they all seem to lose their luster and become just like what had gone before. It's a bit like that favorite song you heard as a kid on the Top 40 station. After hearing the same chorus 3,000 times you knew it by heart and were ready for something else, something with a beat, something you could dance to. Before long those golden oldies were just old.

The same thing is true when you remain in one spot after your welcome is too well worn. That place that was once fresh and clean begins to cloud the air with the acrid scent of the end of the road. In my world, the end of the road is the place where you lay down your head and do the big sleep.

Any given spot only offers only so much to see, so much excitement, so many fun characters and bizarre tales. My theory has always been that if I want to be amused I'm going to have to amuse myself. That works fairly well, but it does to lead to a lot of wear and tear on both the tires and the heart. This same theory has also applied to the women in my life, but let's not talk about that just now. It's a somewhat amusing subject in itself, but only over drinks. Later.

On the other hand, much as I hate admitting it, there does seem to be an exception to every rule. Generalizing about a subject can get a body in a heap of trouble, which is something of a generalization in itself. I found the exception when, to my amazement I one day inadvertently saw myself wandering into a part of the planet that still strikes me as just as weird and wild as the February afternoon I arrived. I figured I'd always be a rolling stone, a goose chaser, a dancer of rainbows. I think I still am, but I'm doing those things all in the same place. This was unexpected, which just goes to show that if the unexpected didn't exist life would be one colossal bore.

The people are happy in this little bump on the earth's crust, the attitude is one of complete kindness and courtesy balanced out with the largest superiority complex I've ever met. These folks call a spade a spade, their mind-set is a mesh of utter solitude and raucous hell-raising. Combine that with soaring peaks, raging creeks, insane weather and a hefty portion of bear and elk and eagle, and you just might find that your soul has been stolen completely away.

The deer and the antelope still play in Montana. So do the residents. So do I.

Here in the mountains, way out west and far from cities and noise and folks who couldn't tell you the truth if it jumped out of their mouth and bit them on the end of the nose, I am light years from the fields and trees and Missouri hills of my birth. I'm even farther from the sun-baked beaches of down south which I never truly called home. The way it looks, I may never leave.

This is a vast and beautiful nation we live in, and as I've covered a bunch of it, I figure I've as much right to compare and contrast as the next guy. Most places have their charms, I'll give you that, but they don't have them all the time. Montana does. Nothing compares to this, although many places do try.

Down south you will find miles of white sand and bikini clad girls. The Florida sunshine can lead you to paradise paralysis. The non-stop life force of New Orleans can rot your brain and age you before your time and make you thank it for the experience. The Ozarks have their tree-covered hills and their hair covered hillbillies, both of which can make you smile at the drop of a hat. Kansas City can suck you in with fountains and barbecue. Virginia is for lovers, that's the God's honest truth, and an Arkansas accent delivered from a tall blonde in cut-offs can send a man on his deathbed into a state of flat-out lust.

There are a thousand good places in this country, and I suppose on the flip-side there are a thousand bad. Still, I've only found one that keeps it's twinkle 365 days a year, and that's in the spot I'm sitting right now.

At this moment I'm tending the fire seven miles back in the Tobacco Root Mountains. For those of you who don't feel the urge to pull out the Rand McNalley, that's about 100 miles northwest of Yellowstone

Park. I've got neighbors who keep to themselves but would give you the shirt off their back. I've got deer and coyote, elk and eagle in the backyard, and have on occasion even had the wandering moose, badger, red fox or black bear stop by for a visit.

My adopted valley of the northern Rockies doesn't have many people, maybe 100 or so on a busy day, so we're pretty far spread out. That's a good thing, and when we feel the need to get together all we have to do is wander down the road for a few laughs and a few beers. It's a good life, but it's not for everybody. Luckily, it's good for me.

I don't have TV that's worth a damn, and the only time I hear a radio station is when I have to drive over the hill to Bozeman or Butte for supplies. I've been met here with nothing but kindness and laughter and good conversation. Maybe there are too many people moving into the west, that's the big fear of the moment, and maybe someday it will be cluttered up with folks who don't have the good sense to lose their uncivilized city ways before they get here. Hell, maybe I've even added to the problem, but I don't think so.

What I do think is that there is no grander place on the planet.

I've come to realize that the end of the road doesn't necessarily lie in the place you stop. Sometimes that stopping point is just the fork that allows you to embark on a whole new beginning. Maybe someday my itchy feet will flare up again and I'll have to point the compass at the setting sun and start walking. I suppose anything's possible, but such a scenario doesn't seem likely. The travel brochures like to call this part of Montana "the last best place." That's corny, but it's also true. It's the best place, anyway. I won't know about the last until the joyride is finished.

Eventually the large percentage of us find a place to light. Unfortunately a very small percentage of us are satisfied with the life we choose. That's a shame, and I think it has something to do with pioneer spirit. A lot of folks just lay down after awhile. They get tired of looking for something better. They become afraid that they will be alone. They settle, giving up their dreams, and are forced to live out their days with the nagging thought that paradise might have been lurking just over the next hill.

Pioneer spirit isn't dead, but it's not nearly as available a commodity as it was in years past. Somewhere along the line life became too easy, too safe, too controlled. People forgot there was a difference between living and existing.

If you want to truly enjoy this eyeblink of existence, you've got to take some risks. You may fail. You may get squashed. Knowing such a fact is the single item that can allow you to stay sharp and succeed. The bigger the risk, the bigger the potential reward. You can't win if you don't play, and those who don't play must resign themselves to sit in the stands and be a passive observer. Go big or go home. Lead, follow or get the hell out of the way. There are clichés galore to define this concept. Maybe the best one begins with waking up.

Last I heard, the Sumner Tavern still sits in its same spot as two decades ago. I'd bet money that, if she's alive, Doris is wielding a Louisville Slugger from behind the bar. Cole Paulson is still a biologist, settled down in a little town and working at an analytical chemistry lab. He hunts and fishes whenever he can, takes one day at a time and smiles often when we speak. Quick Roberts lives in the same town as Cole. He actually did become an artist, as well as a husband and father. Both are doing well, both have moments of wildfire in their eyes just like in the old days. We don't speak nearly as often as in years past, but when we do I can hear humor and life in their voices. They went one way and I went another. That's how life works out. You do what you can to be happy.

I'm happy right now, surrounded by 11,000 foot mountains all white with new snow and a 40 mile per hour wind beating at the doors. It's 20° below zero outside. The samoyed and the husky are crashed out in front of the stove. I wouldn't trade this life for anything.

I'm also betting the four story concrete Canadian Goose is waiting in Sumner, Missouri. Some will see it and laugh, think it the silly idea of a silly little town. Others will look at it and think. They will glance up at the sky, and no matter the season, hear a honking deep in their mind. They will follow where the wild goose takes them. That's what I did.

Of course, it took a long time to get here. There were more than a few stops along the way. Some were good, some were bad and some were so hideously ugly as to nauseate the Gorgon. I'm here now, that's all that matters. I don't know where the end of the road may be, and wouldn't tell you even if I did. Frankly, that knowledge would take all the fun out of the ride.

On the other hand, maybe I can give you some general directions. Maybe I can tell you a few tales from the western road and steer you in the direction of the wild geese.

Listen close, and maybe I can hum you a few bars of coyote song.

Coyote Songs

Tales From The Western Road

Summer Of The Whale

*T*he pilot whale burst forth from the Gulf as if fired from the archer's bow, a shimmering midnight arrow which hung motionless for one eternal second before crashing downward in a ferocious blast of saltwater and raw power. He was long and sleek, perhaps 600 yards from where I lay on the beach. He was straight and true and wild as an exploding star. He was untamed and free. He was beautiful.

Engaging in what had become a mandatory Saturday morn escape from reality, encouraging tan and melanoma, not so surreptitiously admiring the angelic forms of bikini clad young nubiles, I remember that day well. It was the best day of the finest summer. It was the summer of hot looks and cool drinks and the philosophy of manana. It was the only summer I really felt at home with heat and wind and water, forgetting business and worry and other baggage which I did not jettison permanently until I came to these mountains. It was carefree and lazy, the biggest concern of that brief and lovely mindset being the distance to The Beach Club, a plate of half shell oysters and a slab of Key Lime pie.

I call it the summer of the whale.

Some friends joined me there by the pier that day, and I described the vision which, just minutes before, had come within a fraction of reaching escape velocity. "Right Ron," they said, shaking their heads and abjectly failing to conceal amusement at the beach bum's musings. "Sure…we believe you. We'll have what you're having."

Again, as if to stem the condescending note of disbelief, the whale shot once more toward the heavens. The normal hordes of people had arrived by this time, and the pier was beginning to fill with the lemming-esque rampage of northeastern Yankee touristas. You could hear the Oooohs and Aaaahs a thousand yards away. I thought the pier would tip over as the fish-belly-white Yanks shifted en masse to the northern railing for a better view.

My friend Janet yelled, "What the hell was that?"

"Whale," I smiled knowingly.

For a minute we were worried. This was the summer when half a dozen pods of whales inadvertently beached themselves on the barrier islands, which for a whale is a virtual death sentence. Why whales do this, no one truly knows. Some people say their gyroscopes get fouled up, others say it's a bacteria which causes the whale version of a migraine. Some say it's a sort of whale depression which leads to a underwater mammalian suicide pack. Kevorkian would love that one, but I think it's a whale of a tale.

We were scared. With the whale's two appearances, a total of five seconds which have remained in my mind for years, that most wondrous deepwater denizen became ours and ours alone. Whales do not come so close to shore when healthy, at least not most whales, and I sent a silent whisper across the waves.

"Go home," I pleaded.

And with that, I kid you not, the whale made a third brief appearance and headed toward the Texas coast, or perhaps the Yucatan or perhaps some other secret and deep place where whales share secrets. He was safe, and we were blessed forever with his visit.

I got a taste of freedom, of what life could be, during the summer of the whale, but it took many more years before such feelings would grow and prosper. You can't force such things, I know that, and like the whale, you go where your instinct demands.

I will never forget that rocketing black jet, that brilliant work of nature's art, as he shook and sprayed and tore the gentle waves asunder. To me, he symbolized what it all means, or what it might mean if allowed. We all share that same untamed spirit. All we need do is grant acknowledgment.

Yesterday, taking advantage of the unseasonably warm weather, I ventured down to the river for a quiet afternoon's fishing. I could have stayed home, I should have been working. Still, when the mercury rises nearly 100° above it's mark of just a week and a half before, when the promise of spring pokes it's nose out of the cloudless sky with a wink and a smile, it is the wise man who chucks responsibility and seeks out beauty. Work can wait, February days such as this come but rarely. Much like wandering whales and curious cats, the need to enjoy the sheer simplicity of an awakening world takes top priority over the more mundane aspects of life.

Yesterday I saw an eagle in The Bear Trap Canyon. He appeared suddenly, skimming barely twenty feet above the river. He startled me with his brilliance and grace. He spied me in his search for lunch, cocked his head, and beat the air with powerful wings which know no bounds. He was beautiful. He was wild. he was free.

And just for the briefest of seconds, I could swear I saw the whale.

Crystal Balls...Crystal Clear

*T*he beautiful psychic stared deep, those gorgeous eyes taking my interest away from the story I was writing and transporting me into a far more hormonal state of mind. Her voice was husky and soft, blending perfectly with the pungent aroma of sandalwood incense. The wind chimes calmed as she spoke.

"You will move to the mountains. You will write books," she said, flashing a brilliant smile which proved the perfect counterpart to her flowing mane of black hair.

Of course, this was in the days before I developed a ridiculous addiction to six foot tall blondes, or to be more specific, 5'10" and above tall blondes. I wouldn't want to be too restrictive on matters as trivial as height, for one should always keep their options alive. Why...lately I've even found myself eyeing brunettes, not to mention redheads. Blame it on the altitude and too much time with the dog

"Definitely the mountains," she said, laughing a knowing chuckle and tossing back a stray lock which had drifted past her eye. "And, I see books."

Being the cynic, and at this time living below sea level down south in Margaritaville, I took it all with a large box of Mr. Morton's finest sodium. I'm not much into mumbo jumbo or hoodoo voodoo or the prancing, trancing, deadly serious ways so common to most who spend quality time in Dimension X. Nothing against it, in fact I've spent an inordinate amount of my writing life checking, into such claims in an attempt to disprove and humiliate. My brain rents out a couple of cubicles to personalities fascinated by both the unknown and con artists, and I'm drawn to such tangents in the same, way I'm drawn to hanging around smelly midways and yakking with toothless carnie workers. Dark side stuff…without question. A glimpse at the aspect of life which is light years removed from the mundane and common.

"Yes, the mountains," she repeated one last time, "and books."

I laughed to myself, and considered the financial ramifications of starting a snow shovel business in hell. No, not this day, for I definitely heard Willard Scott claim that it was just as warm in Hades as usual. Not freezing over yet, not even frost on the pumpkin, assuming they grow pumpkins in Lucifer Land. I went on my merry way, carrying the image of gorgeous eyes, flashing smile, etc. etc. etc.

Eventually the beautiful psychic and I, as you might have guessed, fell into a very torrid and short lived romance. Two different people from two different worlds who, in retrospect, felt a need to take a dive into strange fields. Our time together was wonderful and weird and eventually drug itself out long past its life span. We've lost touch over the years, but I still think of her from time to time. Mostly I think of her when I look out my front window.

Sitting here' on the third vertebra of the backbone of the world, it requires but one glance at the snow capped peaks to make me feel as if I live at the pinnacle of the planet. Above the trials and tribulations of the flatlanders, sharing space with eagle, bear and elk, I feel we are somehow blessed. It is easy to forget society here, and my only regret is in appearing so late. I know the world encroaches. I know that my revelry and contemplation must eventually switch gears to consider the pains of growth and population. But not yet, just a little more time please.

Perhaps it takes many things to mold a life, many years to decipher the road signs and compass points which lead to a destination, or in keeping with the tone of this tale, predestination. I imagine what it was like here 10, 50, 100 years ago, and discover that even imagination has limits. It's beautiful now, almost beyond belief. Mental conjuring cannot do justice to what it must have been like then. Still, I'm more than satisfied. Hell, lets, be blunt. I'm turning cartwheels.

But. like I said, I've never held much truck with tarot cards and tea leaves and goat guts and such. Intrigued and curious, no doubt, but reality is more quirky and fascinating than anything that could feasibly crop up in a crystal ball. To me, metaphysical musings are a little like dandruff. They don't do any damage and if you get a kick out of spending time and money fiddling with the stuff, so be it. Knock yourself out. Besides, some predictions turn out quite well.

"You will move to the mountains. You will write books."

Thank goodness for beautiful psychics. They make the world a better place. Whether her half correct prediction was lucky guess or some fleeting glimpse into the future, I do not know. What's more, I do not care. I'm here, that's all that matters. I hope her future, as well as her present, is equally bright.

I light a stick of sandalwood incense and look one last time at the peaks, lit majestically by the last fading rays of a dying sun. The view brings a grin, the past brings a smile, and I say once more, thank goodness for beautiful psychics.

But even more, thank goodness for right now.

Hermits

*G*ive me a plot of land on a tree covered hill, a place where wood smoke clings to the branches and the closest neighbor can barely hear the sound of my 30-30 pistol. Give me a little house with a little porch, someplace where I can sit under the night stars, listening to the wind's journey and enjoying a smoke while the wolfhound begs for a scratch behind the ear. Give me a creek with a few fish, or failing that, a pond crowded with skeletal brush. Give me a herd of monster size puppies, a fishing rod, a good book and a lamp. Give me a half decent road, enormous isolation, a desk upon which to write and the crash of an animal through the underbrush.

You want to know my idea of paradise? Welcome to Hermit's Heaven.

The word hermit has a bad connotation. It brings to mind images of stringy haired old men with curling yellow fingernails, creatures devoid of all but three or four teeth who despise their own species and drool into an evening bowl of cold pork and beans. It is a vision of an anti-social miscreant with little use for himself or others, a hobbling cretin in tattered rags who mutters to himself and kicks cats. A hermit is often thought of as a person who, plain and simple, hates life.

Nothing could be further from the truth. Loony toon folks who hear voices in their beanie-weenies and rarely bathe do not have the hermit bent. They may have a short in their brain, but let's not confuse mental disease and improper hygiene with heartfelt desire and an exploratory mind set. Hermits, you see, are simply following their own nature. Crazy people are just crazy.

I've had the opportunity to know several hermits, and without exception all shared an affinity for living beyond compare. They are well traveled and gregarious with a thirst for knowledge. They shower, they speak, and most of all, they learn. They are for the most part kind hearted, with a group of scattered close friends whom they consider family. They like people, but do not feel the compulsion to be constantly surrounded, making idle chit-chat for the sake of hearing their own head rattle. They may have a love of silence and solitude, but they also love life. The difference, is that their method of expression is different from the norm.

Are they odd? Usually, at least if judged by the status quo. Do they care? Not really.

I have been a hermit for as long as I can remember. From the time when I was five or six I could most likely be found either alone on the pond dam (ostensibly in search of catfish but really in another dimension) or off wandering the farm with Skipper the beagle. Solitude gives time to think, time to try and understand our existence so that we may better enjoy it. Hermits, contrary to popular belief, have not necessarily suffered some great and tragic loss which spurs them to withdraw from society and the things of man. In many cases they are merely amazed by (Simon and Garfunkel please forgive me) the sounds of silence. It is the quiet, the absence of TV commercials, billboards, roaring engines and those who hustle and bustle which makes them feel truly at peace. It is the calm that arrives with such peace that lets them venture into the world and be further amazed.

Friends in my past have been, and still are, at a loss to understand my hermit desires. They could not/cannot comprehend the desire to, often, be alone. At one point I reached a stage where I would make up false "prior engagements" just to avoid the inevitable cry of "Why...we can't have you being by yourself." Now I rarely bother. Montana has been good for the honesty genes. It's a take it or leave it kind of place, and I'm glad I took it. It's the only locale where I've ever been able to be myself, also take it or leave it.

People still occasionally comment that I'm getting older, that my dog won't live forever or that I may be missing out on the joys of marriage and family. I respond that age is a state of mind, that, when the sad time comes, I will get another dog. As to the last, the inclination does not seem to be strongly within me. While it has appeared on a couple of occasions, events or personalities (Luckily, I think, for both of us!) have negated the possibility. It's not a consideration at this time, and therefore not worthy of discussion. Some say that's selfish. I say it's honesty to self. Different yokes for different blokes.

One good Chinese curse is "may you lead an interesting life." I do not view such as a curse in the least. The goal of life is to live it as you choose and to live it well; to do otherwise is to cheat yourself and all those with whom you share close association. We should be wise enough to give ourselves the freedom to follow our own roads.

So give me a few acres where the view lasts into tomorrow, a place where the clouds say hello and the eagles scream songs of yesterday. Give me a little house with a little porch, someplace where I can traverse entire galaxies without leaving my chair, where ideas can flood my mind and be transferred to the eyes of those who turn the page. Give me the strength to be myself and the sight to see simplicity. Give me a dozen slobbering wolfhounds, a leaping trout, a good book and a lamp. Give me solitude and time, and I will repay it with joy and appreciation.

I may not have reached Hermit's Heaven just yet, but I'm certainly enjoying the ride.

Dog's Life

My life is a litany of dogs. Some have been timid as mice in therapy, jumping and lurching at the rattlesnake crackle of unfurled Reynolds Wrap or the air rifle pop of a snap-top Dr. Pepper. Others would snarl and lunge, baring small fangs and baying with abandon at carnivorous animals twice, thrice or even four times their mass. Some of my dogs have preferred people and home, the quiet security of sanctuary. Others have existed for the tang of ice air in warm lung and acrid iron of bloody lip. Some sought kind words and gentle scratches, others preferred atavistic growls and drawn fangs.

Dogs are like that. One to the other, minute to minute, you just never know.

People are like that too, albeit far less trustworthy in motive and deed.

In my early days, Tiger the Beagle roamed the fields and forests of south Missouri. He joined me in the construction of straw-walled kingdoms—Bucephalus to my Alexander—as we rode roughshod over infidel fiefdoms in Grandma Jensen's hay barn. Tiger taught me imagination.

The second beagle, Skipper the bold, delighted in the kill, leaving rabbits, sparrows and live bluegill on the front step before I would wander down to the gravel road to meet the big yellow bus. Skipper taught me self reliance.

Crow the Labrador was a psychic and a genius, imparting life and Frisbee with the wisdom of a beach bound Buddhist. B.J. the Rottweiler was a prisoner—emancipated from a tyrant master by midnight's blackness—who chose to perish with honor and dignity. Crow taught me wonder. B.J. taught me sacrifice.

Then there is Buffett the Wolfhound, kind and gentle yet six feet tall and deadly loyal. Henry, my little red dog, picked me from a line-up. We came home from the pound, he hopped on the bed, and the smiles have never faded for a moment. By a brief marriage (or rather, by a quick divorce) I have also inherited full rights to an ancient warrior Samoyed. We now run together. The trio possess things I've yet to learn.

The point of this rant? I suppose it is to illuminate the incongruity between dogs and people, the fact that canine insight demands care only of important stuff. I'm mystified at how humans become inflamed and venomous over minutia such as politics and current events, when their attention should be focused on their own lives and freedoms. I'm astonished at those who believe that all is crisis, who are unaware that the lying emissaries from Planet Hollywood seek only self aggrandizement. Don't folks know it's a scam?

Maybe I don't understand. I'm thankful for that,

I rarely write about writing. In fact, I've never written about writing before and, best guess, probably never shall again. It is boring for all save he who puts the words in a decipherable sequence. It is not romantic, despite the claims of the biographers who chronicle the transient existences of fabled scribblers. More times than not it is a profession borne of inflated ego and invective adoration.

Writers are not journalists—that's a different profession entirely. Succinctly, journalists record and writers create. The latter, whether through the guise of fiction, non-fiction, essay or sonnet, exist to offer up their own opinion. To present even the most obscure suggestion of an objective accounting would be labeled as transparent pretense.

Like dogs, we sniff the scent in the air. If the scent be pleasing we grin, yapping in a high pitch and bouncing about the yard. If the scent be foul, we expose teeth and prowl, seeking soft underbelly for the damaging bite.

That's what I do. Then again, my life has been a litany of dogs, and dogs are more human than most humans. I like poking fun, considering and thinking. You jab, back off, laugh, and jab again. Most of the serious issues of the day fail to be serious once given a few minutes thought, and pale in comparison to family, friends, canines or whether or not the ribs are burning.

But that's just me, a mountain lovin' purveyor of prose who believes life begins and ends at home and the rest is fodder for the jocularity mill. I learn from things close, not from talking heads or printing press, and feel all who take issue with common sense, whose fearful brains accept only that which is popular or safe, suffer from severe humor impairment.

Of course, since I'm not pretending to be ultra-serious and mega-concerned about every issue from gays in the rain forests to wolves on the picket line, the humor impaired label me apathetic, arrogant, warped, soul-less and cynical. They rant, rave and write long nonsensical letters. They sweat, stutter and leave five minute phone messages of unintelligible garble.

I assume such folks are bored, and generally trash their hard worn efforts after enjoying the first apoplectic sentence. The dogs find such stuff highly amusing—calling up all their friends to share the oddness—but realize there are matters of far greater consequence, like their own lives, the lives of their kin, and the hope that Ron didn't burn the aforementioned ribs.

Being dogs, they don't understand obsession with mass consumption triviality. The prefer laughing reality.

So do I.

Hope's Eternal Spring

I believe in long tall English blondes, the restorative power of Mark Twain and the imposing sanctity of a raging river. I believe that one should never covet their neighbor's power tools, that all dogs go to heaven, and that Elvis works in a downtown Minneapolis Burger King. I believe in highs and lows, rains and snows, dogs named Crow and that you love what you know. I believe in a lot of things. Mostly I believe in the impossible. Mostly, I believe in hope.

Mostly, I believe in Spring.

Spring is the season of the impossible, the era of new beginnings. Its sudden, green-shooted arrival allows a brief glimpse into the universal maybe, a gaze into the abyss of potential. Spring is when hope rings eternal, and when eternity screams of hope. It is the time when even the most reclusive of hermits shed their skins and make a tentative foray into the wilds of society and the crevices of mind. They wander beyond their usual and familiar haunts, those hidden places where safety is defined by comfortable surroundings and trustworthy intimates, on a Grail quest through unknown territory. Though the alarm bells may ring, the blood pressure rise, the maps scream out with their veiled warning of "Here There Be Tigers," Spring offers the courage to persevere. Such is but one of its many gifts to man.

Spring is nature's version of the I Ching, a Tarot deck clothed in sunny skies, lightning storms, sudden snows and the birth of wild things. It is astrology from above the tree line, a forecast dealing not with symbols and signs and numbers, but rather with reality. It is before your eyes, if you will but observe. It is the big print version of the Book of Life. For the next installment, merely turn the page.

I sometimes feel for those who live in the far southern lands, my former home of sun, surf and sand, for they cannot experience the quiet explosion that is a mountain spring. Beautiful is Margaritaville, no doubt, but it's just not the same. There, Spring is virtually indiscernible from Winter, Summer, or Fall. Live long enough in that sensually tropical, albeit monochromatic climate, and it will eventually come to pass that you gain an inkling of the change of seasons, but the sensation is more internal that outwardly apparent.

Perhaps the inner tingles are merely the yearnings of the body clock, an amazing and all knowing biological Timex which informs that, somewhere, someplace, all is new again. Perhaps that quiet pull is the legend of instinct, a need to break with things which have served their time, repair that which is broken, replace the used, consider the alternatives, rekindle simmering coals which refuse to lose their fire. Perhaps…

We should never take Spring for granted, just as we should guard at all costs against failing to gaze longingly at our wondrous ice-carved mountains, dip our feet in the frigid run-off of the Madison River, stop for a moment and inhale deep the fragrant smells of trees and flowers and grass. Never should we forego the chance to send good wishes to the antelope which line our roads, preparing to give birth to new life. That we see them every day is our good fortune, and good fortune should not go unthanked or ignored. Always should we step outward under our endless dome of night, throw wide our arms and shout words of amazement toward the heavens. Forever should we wander back into the canyon and scream yet again, waiting but seconds for the enthusiastic echo to respond in whole-hearted agreement at the miracle. It is Spring, and suddenly, I am filled with belief.

For instance, I believe that words are song and that love never dies. I believe in a flaming sunrise, the dance of a sandhill crane and the graceful leap of a whitetail. I believe that the years are long but time is short, that miles are but minutes and that, in Spring, hope is another name for tomorrow.

I believe in a lot of things. Mostly, I believe that nothing is more possible than the impossible.

Mostly, I believe that to ignore this most special of times is to ignore ourselves.

Mostly, I believe that to hold onto hope is to live life to the fullest.

Mostly, I believe in Spring

Surprise

*I*t is the calm after the storm I cherish, not the lull before. The anticipation of before bothers me, for I arrogantly assume the most likely outcome, yet nonetheless am forced to wait for fruition. It is the cosmic equivalent of a nervous tick, a personal character quirk. Will the hopes equal the reality?

The anticipation of after is much less gentle in its caress, but all the more invigorating for its mystery. In that post storm uncertainty, when the rattles and bangs and crashes have sought out new quarters, there is both calm and fire. Uncertainty reigns supreme. The sum of all potential lies in the after. What's next?

Lets see it! Lets do it! Lets rock! Not a patient soul, this expatriate beach bum/farm boy/teller of small tales. Not a believer in subtlety for the sake of social posturing. I want the unknown, the novel, the surprising, the true; something that brings an uncontrolled laugh, a neck wrenching twist of the head, a startled jump, or maybe best of all, a smiling warmth which penetrates cells, corpuscles and shoe leather.

Then again, don't we all?

The reward of patience is patience. I believe St. Augustine of Hippo said that, which makes me a little suspect of the phrase's validity right off. St. Auggie was neither patient nor saintly, at least in his younger days, and his passionless, unrealistic (and no fun) view of relations between the sexes has tainted society for 1,600 years! Let's face it, Auggie would have thought Queen Victoria was a slut!

Still, it's a good line, whoever holds first muttering rights, and a trait I've been trying to learn. Or, more honest, a trait which I've been trying to decide if I should try to learn.

This will sound garishly metaphysical, but I often feel that the base nature of the human animal, patience as well as its antithesis, is found in the storms. They seem a reflection, or perhaps more suiting, an atmospheric diorama, of our various moods. The gentle rains, the icy mists, the lightning, thunder and ill winds...all these things are as familiar to human behavior as they are to meteorology, and no more predictable. A sunny day can burn you, a sudden mountain snow can chill dusk's seductive warmth. The winds can blow and roar and shake loose the shutters, and in their wake leave a peace which you have never before imagined.

Unpredictable. Wonderful. And, in retrospect, I think, not the place for patience.

Patience is simply not the correct word, an inadequate mind set. A third cousin maybe, but how can one suggest patience when contemplating those things which are uncontrollable? It's more of an eager ambivalence, forgetting anticipation and accepting graciously what comes. Nature will take its course, undoubtedly, and we can do nothing but wait quietly for the outcome. The effect of cloud seedings are rather short term, in the long haul their effect is minimal.

Once, when much younger and probably only a bit more dense, I told a friend that I could rarely recall being surprised. Here, in the high lands, the surprise is that I ever felt that way to begin with. It is but one of a million surprises which occur each day, as simple as forgetting fear, throwing arms wide, and opening your eyes to unlimited possibilities.

With that thought in mind, I will strive to enjoy the calm before as well as the calm after. Both are gifts far beyond my paltry comprehension. Each are different, each are equal, and arrogance has no place in the contemplation of things unknown. Both should be a joy.

And they are.

Civilization

I would not give you a plugged nickel for a city. They are full of cars and people and a certain unwashed arrogance which I find offensive. They are often smug places, the air inevitably filled with the condescending attitude of superiority through numbers. You don't know your neighbors in a city, unless they call the cops because your music is too loud or you turn out to be a serial killer or something. You can't see antelope in a city (right now there are 40 on the second bench behind my house) unless you visit some pre-Cambrian zoo and watch the suckers pacing endlessly in small, tight pens. The people who live in these urban conglomerates of fast paced thoughts and unlimited reproduction seem penned as well, adopting an isolationist policy in regards to all who do not possess password and proper credentials. It's a closed club, one whose membership requirements are not to my liking.

I have never seen the slightest trace of civilization in a city. I've seen cultural events and technological doo-dads and the very latest in fashion trends, but such is not my definition of civilization. To be civilized means stopping to help a neighbor change a tire in the same manner you would help an uncle or cousin. To be civilized is to wave at cars you pass on the road, to smile and say hello as you walk down main street. Courtesy is the bedrock of civilization, I think, the grease which keeps the wheels of a healthy society from being jammed with sand and grit. We may not have ballet or rock concerts or cable TV here in the Madison Valley, but we've got oodles of courtesy.

Stop and help change a tire in a city…are you kidding? Not unless my prized 30-30 pistol is loaded and at the ready. Smile on the streets of a city…forget it? Making eye contact could lead to a mugging, not to mention particularly nasty puncture wounds. Say good morning just for the reason of sharing the day? People would view you as a nut.

What a shame it is, and how fortunate we are.

A friend of mine says that the higher you go, the more civilized life becomes. I think he is right. Our distances, our individuality, allow us to appreciate human interaction to a higher degree than those who are packed wall to wall in an insane asylum of exhaust fumes and concrete and squirming flesh. Our sense of place, our sense of home, prepare us to treat each other (usually) with respect and kindness.

Strange words, I know, coming from one of the hermit bent, but true nonetheless. Rare is the time when I will travel further than the canyon or the mountain meadows (unless you count the Bear Claw Bar & Grill, which you can't because I've adopted the middle bar stool as my favorite doing business place) for I find solitude and the wild cries much more civilized than any creation of man. My relationships with people are oftentimes strained and tentative and fractious. My relationships with a dog and a stream and an eagle are easy and relaxed.

You do not have to explain yourself to the mountain, and generally feel no desire to attempt such a thing. Even if you tried, if you went crazy and the urge became overwhelming, the mountain would ignore you. Those who were born here seem to know this fact internally. Those of us who came here later either sensed it, learned it or left.

I feel winter on the horizon, eagerly anticipate a bone chilling wind and the sight of snow flakes in the night sky. It is simple, and in simplicity lies civilization. Truth, beauty, honesty… the elements which are found in the wild—sometimes violent beyond words, sometimes gentle as early morning dew—are gifts which we have graciously been given. Appreciating these things, seeing them as a wonder rather than a nuisance, is what makes this place more civilized than most any other I have encountered.

I would not give you a plugged nickel for a city.

I would not take millions for here.

Winter

*T*he cacophonous song of low flying honkers might have said it better, the distant bugling of amorous elk might have said it louder, but nothing spoke more clearly than that first glimpse of white-topped mountain. It spoke of the promise of the seasons. A more violent, more rugged, yet somehow more gentle time was on the horizon. I, for one, was glad.

Perhaps winter isn't the best of seasons, maybe no better than spring, summer or fall. All hold their own mysteries and fascinations, and the beginning of each never fails to bring a quickening to the pulse and a lump to the throat. Who knows the reason. It might be something as simple as a sense of change, something in the grand design which throws us into new modes of thought and behavior just as the soul starts to itch and the doldrums hit high fever. Man cannot live by bread alone. Neither can he live (well) with the monotony of a solo climate. It might be something as complex as biological memory, a forgotten remembrance of old instincts and ancestral motivations which linger somewhere in our synaptic pathways, tempting us to howl or burrow or sleep. It might be a lot of things. The only thing we can say for certain is that winter looms just over the horizon, certain and unyielding and full of mystery.

Still, and although I will most likely choke on these words by the end of February, winter has become my favorite part of the year. More solid than the other seasons, stubborn and relentless and egocentric as hell, winter is the shrill rantings of a small child who will not quiet, the barking dog who remains out of boot range. It is recalcitrant lovers and a glimpse through mortality's portal. It is that, and more.

The vision of a silent curtain of white stuff, frosty tears dripping from twilight eyes, creates an air of myth and reverence. Before long the clang of swords will begin in Valhalla, the sparks from the Norsemen's epic battles once again floating softly downward to coat Mother Earth in a blanket of white. The bone-chilling wind, it's banshee howl railing against glass and wood (and sometimes flesh) brings us into close encounters of the meteorological kind which are unknown in more moderate climes. Winter is real, a tangible presence, something to which one must acquiesce graciously or remain forever frustrated. Old King Canute could not order back the tide, neither can we raise the Fahrenheit. In winter, even the mercury sleeps. I welcome it.

Of course, it was not always this way. Not so many years ago I would lie on a winter beach, soaking up tan, running for the coat closet should the temperature hit 65°. That seems a lifetime ago, and maybe it was. I didn't know how deeply I missed the change. I didn't know what it meant. You see, it is not just the snow and the cold and the slate-gray sky I cherish. It is something more personal.

Winter, for we who live here, is our time. The hectic pace of summer is gone. The Winnebagos and Air Streams do not crowd the roads, the foreign plates remain in foreign lands. The hills are alive with the sound of silence, and for me, contemplation sets in. I like the cold-dark times because I often have a cold-dark nature. Winter is solitude and books and dead quiet. Nostalgia and reflection and plans for the coming of green-shooted life. More than anything, it is a re-charge of the soul and an escape from the madding crowds. Beautiful, this season soon to be. A good time. Our time. My time.

The honkers are honking more regularly now, the elk are looking for dates and making loud elk noises. Their message is clear, they say it well. But, on this mid-September day, a lone, snow-capped peak says it best.

I look to the sky and smile.

Soon, I think. Soon.

Waiting On The Wind

I watch the clouds swirl high over the western peaks and marvel at their magic. Maybe, in an hour or three, they will come ripping down into the valley like a runaway freight train. No Chattanooga Choo Choo this, more like the Wabash Cannonball or the Old 97 in its pre-wreck days. The spectral firemen shovel in the coal, the fire in the boiler licks and jumps and stretches it's white hot fingers towards the twilight dome. Soon the steam will build to a pinnacle, and with a piercing shriek and a shower of sparks, the juggernaut shakes loose it's bonds and descends with the battle cry of the Valkyries.

There is something wild about sitting in the down below and watching the up above. It is the stuff of dreams—forces beyond our reckoning. It is the mystery of the honking V squadrons of geese and the end of the rainbow. The clouds merge and break and seek out new partners in the atmospheric kaleidoscope. They race and laugh and dance the cumulus tango. I do not understand why, which is good, because my attempts to discern the indiscernible generally lead to disappointment and disaster. You see, sometimes I don't want to understand.

"Woe be to the man who seeks too long and too hard after his gods." I read that once in a rag-eared Robert Ripley book. The Ripster had written the caption under his sketch of a Hindu ascetic, a fakir who sat, every day, staring blindly at the sun. His limbs were withered from inactivity, his corneas had long ago been fried in their sockets. Perhaps his mind was gone as well. Still he sat, seeking wisdom, attempting to comprehend the ways of nature and the gods. Maybe he found it. If so, the price seems exorbitant.

I wonder, why must we always attempt to analyze? Sometimes, simple appreciation takes precedence over dissection.

The pursuit of knowledge is a good thing, make no mistake. It is the duty of man to climb the tree and shake off the apples and explore the nooks and crannies of mind and place. To do less is to be sub-human, an amoebae. In this day and age, and I'm sure in days and ages past, many human folk have been too willing to sit complacently and accept the opinions of others. We are told, we believe. Such is not healthy, no matter whether it applies to mathematics or religion or politics or people.

We are not meant to be domesticated animals, we are meant to quest and seek and sate our curiosity. One of the problems with the world is the absence of the decision making gene, the lack of guts and self reliance and a questioning nature in what seems to be an ever-growing percentage of the population. Many prefer that others take care of them, rather than taking care of themselves. They seek convenience without cost, comfort without sacrifice, consensus without wisdom. I do not despise such folks, only pity their lack of intestinal fortitude and misguided perceptions. Man is the creature that shows his teeth when he smiles, not the one who roles over on his belly and bares his neck. The feckless and weak cannot control their lives and thoughts, and thus cannot enjoy the majesty of things uncontrollable.

Perhaps it's a fine wire to walk, knowing when to control, knowing when to acquiesce, but a noble goal all the same. We should never disregard the importance of the unknown, the creative potential that can be unleashed by mystery. We should be wise enough to realize that we are not always in command, that there are some things beyond our ken.

I don't really care to delve into what makes the fire crackle or the whitetail leap. It is not important to me, the scientific explanation behind a twinkling star or haloed moon. When it comes to matters of beauty, and beauty can be anything from croaking frog to a stimulating conversation, it is enough that such things exist. I'm glad that I'm bull-headed enough to sometimes become demanding and obnoxious and weird, but more glad that I'm lazy, awed or dumb enough to, at other times, merely appreciate.

The clouds continue to build, combining their strength for that moment when they will scale the granite fortress and plunge forth in a cascade of white Montana wind. There is a time to be analytical, and a time to let the mind wander. A little magic is good for the soul. It is fine to learn, it is fine to learn to let go.

I sit silently and light a smoke. Sometimes you don't have to be the lead actor in the human drama.

Sometimes it's more fun to just enjoy the show.

Listening For The Light

Some people are like candles, burning brilliantly for the illumination of others while they slowly burn themselves out. Others, more constant in both manner and temperament, could be compared to a river. They flow endlessly in the same basic channel, their currents mirroring storms and tides and the influence of innumerable outside forces. Though the river's waters may boil, rise and recede, eventually they return to their established pace.

I've known folks who reflected both of these attributes to a greater or lessor degree, but it seems the happiest are those born in a harmony between the two extremes. They flare to life in the darkest of times, conserving their strength and passing it along to those who would stumble and fall. They show kindness and concern in the darkest of hours, brightening the way for others while at the same time removing obstacles with a gentle and constant pressure. They do not consume themselves, but rather consume life. In the process they find nourishment rather than hunger, joy rather than sadness, peace rather than conflict.

It is not a question of compromise; I've never subscribed to the theory that the willow is strong because it bends. It is a question of conviction and principal and common sense. Be yourself at all costs, or you will one day discover that the cost to self is exorbitant.

I was thinking about such things the other night, trying to decide just where I could fit into such a scenario. I'm definitely not of the candle mode, for I'm often in the dark. The illumination sought by those of the hermit bent is generally illumination of self, and though we do have a tendency to burn out on occasion, such is where the comparison ends. Similarly, I could find little juxtaposition between self and river. My waters have often split and diverged from the safety of the main channel, heading this way and that, sometimes lying for a time in stagnant pools, at others racing down the mountainside in a frenzied cataract. Neither candle nor river nor combination of the duo am I, a problematic situation that has frequently caused no little consternation to friends, loved ones and acquaintances of both the new and old variety.

In truth I would guess that few of us fit specifically into such well defined categories. Only on the rare occasion do we hear of the soul that is truly stout of limb and sound of mind and pure of heart. It is the stuff of Arthurian legend, and even those valiant knights fell humbly to their knees on a regular basis. It is an infrequent occurrence indeed when we perchance to actually meet such individuals, and even if we do, we tend to ignore their gifts. The true warrior of the spirit is the quiet type, bursting to life when needed, sharing tranquillity and silent lessons and laughter in the manner of the patient teacher and valued friend.

Wisdom does not rush, it treads slowly and speaks softly. It is up to us to either listen or disregard, dependent upon our own needs, desires and ability.

And so, the more I contemplated the situation, I arrived at a conclusion with which I could agree. Candle or river or anything in between matters little. Our personalities are not so important as what we make of them. Our desires are worth far less than the ability to desire. A world full of the all-knowing and all-seeing would be a serious and boring place, and frankly, I like a little confusion and hardship in life. It makes the better times all the better, and with experience, leads us to paths that make the difficult not so bad. It allows us to laugh at ourselves, which may be the greatest weapon man possesses in his struggle with life. Look around. There is plenty to laugh at.

Neither a candle nor river am I, but luckily, there are some that are. Remembering that, I can do nothing but listen for the wisdom of others, watch for the flash of insightful light and attempt to avoid the rocks and whirlpools so prevalent on the uncharted course.

The lighthouse beams and the buoys ring their bells. The messages are there.

It is up to the ears to hear and the eyes to see.

Sunset

*T*he true beauty of the sun, that big yellow ball which has eluded my valley for so much of this summer, comes not with its first morning peek over the eastern horizon or during noontime heat. There are those who would disagree with this, I'm sure, and while such is their prerogative, they are misguided in their beliefs..

Some feel there is virtue in arising with the chickens, rambling about while the dew soaks through still tired feet, waiting in anticipation for the sun to wake and stretch and yawn it's first golden rays toward a slumbering planet. This is dandy for some folks, mostly insomniacs and Amish tribesmen and tortured souls with either an obsessive Puritan work ethic or strong guilt complex, but not for me. Sunrises are beautiful, I'll grant you that, and I would probably watch more of them if they didn't happen before the sun came up. Early to bed and early to rise may have been a slogan which made Ben Franklin a lot of bucks and tightened the curls of persnickety old matrons of pre-Victorian demeanor, but Ben was a notorious ladies man and wee hours party prowler. I'll bet he never opened his eyes before 10:00 a.m., with 2:30 being a more likely choice and only then with a hangover.

Others are devoted worshippers of brown skin and sweat, but these are mostly either pontoon tourists or people who have an aversion to the long admired color of fish-belly white. I've never seen much use to acquiring a tan, but that may be because I spent a number of years living on one of those far south beaches where everybody is automatically tan and exceptionally pretty until that inevitable day when they burn out and get leather-lipped and occasionally fall down in public.

Yes, I was tan in those olden days, roughly the color of a roasted hazelnut, but I was also much younger and dumb enough to view excessive melanin production in the same sense as rum and Hi-Karate after-shave and other alleged pheromone enhancing tools of the universal mating dance. These days I try to avoid tanning not because I worry about malignant melanoma or other nasty skin diseases, but more because I'm old and lazy. Tanning is hard work and generally a group project. I don't do groups. It also requires making small talk and exhibiting social graces, two pastimes for which I have little desire and less talent. Such attributes are beyond the lexicon of non-pretty, leather-lipped hermits with giant dogs who live in a tar paper house and occasionally fall down in public. I prefer to sit in the dark and type, and the money saved on sun-block and light bulbs allows me to engage in necessary activities like paying the rent.

The true beauty of the sun, that big yellow ball which has eluded the valley for so much of this summer, comes not with its first peek over the eastern horizon or during the noontime heat. It comes just before dark.

Frankly, I can't tell you why I enjoy this, but I do. There is a certain quiet to a hot summer night, or even a cool summer night for that matter, that is more peaceful than anything else. I watch the sky turn flaming red, or flaming purple or flaming pink. I see that not-so-hot star in our sky (though hot enough to cook us silly if we're not careful) start to drop behind distant caps of snow. The birds seem louder, the whish of their wings seeming to crackle with energy. The bugs seem quicker, darting here and there in search of skin meals or whatever it is that bugs do when they aren't getting eaten or squashed. The dog wants to play and suddenly I don't give a hoot about ringing phones or dinging doorbells or any of the other day to day menaces that screw up an otherwise fine existence.

I like sunsets. I like them because, unlike sunrises or noontime heat, they have the good sense to just relax and let the day slide away. They do not toil, they do not work, they are simply enjoying themselves. The evening sun knows better than to strive and fight, knows that time is too short to whine about what should have been done or what is left to do.

Our sunsets are limited, all too few in number. I sit on the old school bench above the root cellar, long after the sun is gone from sight and the stars begin to freckle the black dome, and try and appreciate the sense of time, the frailty of our skittering minutes upon this earth, that comes with a summer's evening.

I will no doubt forget what I learn by morning. I'll start thinking too much and worrying over things that mean too little. Still, as the big yellow ball slides into the shadows, even this is not a major problem. All I must do is wait a few hours.

The lesson will be repeated until I get it right.

Terminus

It is a dark and silent night. I've washed the dog, pan-fried one of the last trout from last year's last ice-fishing excursion, and thrown wide doors, windows and soul for a good airing. I sit outside and sniff the air for sign. It seems Fall may be on us very soon. The evenings bring gentle chills and the mornings promise frost. It is a good time of year, and for whatever reason, I feel a rare relaxation, a sense of peace, that has been lacking for most of this peril-filled summer.

There are fewer cars returning from the lake tonight, fewer speed-racers towing fiberglass creations past my rocky plot than just a week ago. There are more birds singing and more quiet. There are yips and howls and wings of creatures large and small brushing the cotton-woods. The grass and weeds still grow, they still think it's high summer, but I know better. We are quickly coming to the change. While some may furrow the brow and bare the teeth at such a notion, while they may dread the shorter days and curse the inevitable bone chilling cold, I am more than ready.

It has been a hard few months for this hermit soul. A summer which has included death and loss and numerous frustrations with which I'll bore you only a bit further. I guess even I have my limits in revealing such stuff, so let's just say that I deal with both death and frustration poorly, and leave it at that. A wandering life creates friendships which last a lifetime, but the very nature of such a choice makes those bonds occur all too seldom. No complaints, never. No regrets either. Still, when one of those bonds is broken, whether by freak accident or the process of nature, emotional sense tends to take a sabbatical and a hazy blackness dries the joy of everyday things faster than July sun on morning dew.

I don't even call it depression, just my own method of mourning, or perhaps an attempt to sort out what it all means. Whatever the case, the sad feelings of this summer have led me to rants and raves and rages which vary in degree from the silent brood to the public outrage. The tongue lashes out and the pen stings. The sweat pours and the mind screams and you hope that folks understand and put up with it.

Finally, you figure out that it is time to let go and get on with the business of living.

Jimmy Buffett is singing an island lullaby in the background, something about being ruled by antiquity and inconsistency, which I find ironically fitting for this moment. It is hard to break patterns, difficult to reach down and tug on the bootstraps and venture back into the world at large. We are creatures of habit, and some of us take refuge in those dark caves in which we find protection and solace. Still, one must eventually pop up their head and peek over the edge of the foxhole. Life is a battle, and while it can be a joyous struggle, it is nonetheless hand to hand combat complete with its losses, victories and stalemates. Sometimes the strategy must be to let go of affronts (whether supposed or real) tragedies and anger. Sometimes, the best plot and the wisest scheme is to admit that our destiny is rarely of our own design. Sometimes the best offense is strategic retreat.

Sometimes, the best revenge against the whims of fate lies in living well.

I suppose I could go on with this philosophical psycho-babble all night long, sometimes I can really wheeze the stuff out. But, as I said, I think maybe it's time to drop some baggage and move on. The dog is sleeping and the sky is so full of clouds that the western peaks are invisible save to imagination. I like it. It's how it was and how it is, and I think, how it should be.

I hear an owl hooting down by the creek. I feel a crisp snap to the air that sings of vitality and the promise of change. I feel a soul striving to reach back into that reservoir of calm so prevalent until such a short time ago. I start to slow down, the clock springs unwind, and I'm reminded of the importance of time. I'm reminded that the demons are powerless over those who can find laughter in the simple things, that we should remember the good, let loose the bad and hold tightly to those things we care for as if every moment is our last. Our days are too few, our time too short, to do anything less.

A cloud slips its skyward track, revealing, for the briefest second, the smiling face of the man in the moon. I listen for the silence one last time before sleep comes, and in that blessed hush hear the beating of my own heart.

It's been too long.

Thrills & Chills

*T*he warm Chinook swept in and quickly melted our newly laid quilt of white stuff, leaving nary a trace save for mud holes and sodden earth and the tracks of my rusty four wheeler in the driveway. Just a few days earlier the skies had opened, first dropping snowman material with a gentle cascade, and later with a marked horizontal pitch. A few days before that it had been so cold that the mercury refused to move, no doubt hiding in its home at the base of thermometer and reading classic novels in front of a roaring blaze. The Jeep coughed and stuttered (and finally caught) not only in the morning, but as well at noon and twilight. The dog didn't even want to venture out, which if you knew my dog would tell you something right off.

So it is and so it goes. My guess is that before this column sees ink, yet another 180° turn will come to pass.

I get tickled talking to my southern friends when it's so cold that the icicles grow from limb to sky rather than vice versa. There is a certain unbelief in their voice, and over the phone lines you can just barely make out a not so imperceptible shaking of the head. "Doesn't it bother you," most of them ask.

"Weather is weather," I say. "it doesn't matter one way or the other. If it's nice I go fishing. If it's too cold I stay inside. If there's snow I pour a glass of wine and enjoy the show. If the roads are slick I simply don't drive."

"I don't see how you can like that," they comment, the noggin shaking increasing by 10 degrees and 40 revolutions per minute.

"But I do," I respond.

That's the explanation I generally offer, the quick and easy way to avoid excess oxygen waste on nice folks who, nevertheless, wouldn't understand. The truth of the matter is that I'm not so concerned about weather as I am variety and spontaneity, and perhaps it's close cousin, the freedom that comes with those two elusive qualities. I like those traits in my weather the same way I like it in the various canines who have hung around throughout my life. They are the attributes that I notice in my closest friends—somewhat eccentric and unpredictable but never boring—and the characteristics that I try (and hopefully sometimes succeed) to inject into my writing.

I bore easily, and since this is a place where I've yet to get bored, it must be a good place. Weather doesn't matter. In fact, active weather is one of the things that prevents me from getting bored. If I wanted the monotone version of climate I'd move to Florida, which is somewhere I once left because, among other reasons, I was bored silly. Now put that logic in your pipe and smoke it.

Oh sure, Florida has tornadoes and hurricanes and escaped road prison inmates. California has earthquakes and mudslides and floods and gang slayings by the oodles. But, there's a difference between spontaneous variety and spontaneous disaster. Those states have good things to offset the bad, granted, but somehow they don't seem as wild and free as the goings on in these parts. I'd much rather hear of a bear in the backyard than a new condo project, am eternally thankful I can sit in my house, six foot dog stretched out on a seven foot couch, and work at something that makes me happy. I won't say I'd wither up and die in the nine to five world, but I'd probably apply for a job with the government so I'd have an excuse when I went crazy and shot up a McDonald's.

I think the case is one of different strokes, and the best way I know to offset that particular brain malady is to do what you like, regardless of money or peer pressure or the curled lips of society at large, in a place that you love. That way you'll never get bored. And, if in a mood of funk you begin, just for a second, to question your decision, all you need do is remember the alternative. Trust me, the smile accompanying that particular epiphany will light up the room.

It's muddy right now and there's a bit of a wind kicking up. Being January, and being Montana, that means a change is right around the corner. It might be another Arctic storm trooper coming to visit, maybe a hurricane force gale, or perhaps some more wandering warmth that took a wrong turn on the interstate. Whatever, it makes no difference. The weather can be anything it damn well pleases. For one thing, it was here first. For another, it's a vitally important part of the package.

I am fond of this package. Its colors change with each sunset, and the wrappings are just as pretty as the contents.

Second Sight

*T*he road snaked towards heaven like a sprig of velvet hair ribbon caught in a Texas twister. Meandering and falling ever upward, disappearing behind sudden turns and even more sudden drops, I felt a few of my own over-tight springs begin to uncoil. Trust me, that doesn't happen very often for a lot of us. At least not in this part of the world. At least not between May and October. At least not during that season when Camcorders are as thick as Caddis flies and coyotes.

Flanked by the velvet spring meadow on one side and the lodegpole pines on another, I had to wonder why. What makes a person forget about the important stuff in life—trees and fish and waking bears, Memorial Day snow banks so deep that they laugh at a 4 wheel drive, an eagle's scream and the sure-footed hop of a mountain goat—and get all obsessed with something as trivial as business? Is money really that important? Would we trade treasures beyond worth for trinkets and baubles and beads?

That's when I understood that I'd lost my way for a little while. Well, maybe not then. Maybe I figured it out just now.

The new spring run-off built its own creek beds in the midst of the rocky path, the bugs hovered above the hidden lake in a fine cloud of dark mesh. I sat there goggle-eyed and wondered why the hell it had taken me so long to go such a short ways.

Just dumb, I reckon. Misplaced priority, I figure.

No more, I said.

I went back to that spot for two consecutive days, and no, I'm not about to say where it was. Anybody who knows me well might be able to figure it out, but since the place has not been one my usual haunts (at least until recently) I doubt even that. I ain't tellin', for I've seen too many different places in too many different states get killed by popularity. It's easy to choke the life out of the golden goose, and getting smothered in dollar bills and neon is a pretty horrid way to go. That's my biggest fear for this place. I wonder if we'll figure it out in time.

A couple of whitetails dashed the road and cleared the creek with barely a puff of breath. Big monsters they were, maybe the biggest I've ever seen. The bald bird swooped down over the surface, and while claws failed to connect with trout, it didn't seem to bother him much. There's always next time. Tomorrow is another day.

It's funny how a mind-set can change. While I do like the spring and summer, that easy ability to toss a line or just lay in the grass and feed the bugs, I've become a winter person in the last few years. You couldn't pay me enough to get on a ski slope—too many people trying to show off their fancy ski wear—but I will dress up in 26 layers of clothes and go up and down the road with monster dog when it's 26° below. I like winter because it brings normalcy. Things slow down, mainly because it's pointless to try and make a fancy impression when your face is beet red and your nose hairs are frozen.

We might get cabin fever in winter, but I'm pretty certain that's better than tourist fever.

My definition of a tourist is not the standard. Anybody who comes here to make a home, and I don't care if they're from Bugtussle or Bulgaria, is welcome in my book. Visitors are also welcome, as long as they don't behave like asses. As long as a person respects this place, doesn't try to change it, melt it down, turn it into some Disneyfied version of what it should be naturally, I could care less. Welcome. Can I buy ya a beer? Better yet, you buy me one.

It's those folks who want to brag to their friends about how they live in the "wilderness" in a $10,000,000 home for two weeks out of the year, the ones who whine and bitch and snarl about the lack of cable TV or snow removal or a McDonalds, that get under my skin. Not knowing the difference between a blue heron and a sandhill crane is fine, those things can be learned. The ones that are just here for the social standing or to make a quick buck, that's the person that I'll most likely swerve for.

I came here to make a home, but as I looked eye to eye with that high mountain, peered at my reflection in the lake, I didn't particularly like what I saw. I saw myself playing it safe, holding back a few thoughts that I would have easily/eagerly voiced a year ago. I was being careful not to offend anybody who might put a buck in my pocket. I either had to find my way back or step off the edge. I was becoming, in a small way, the thing I hated.

Losing your way is all right, as long as you come back to earth. Somehow I forgot that for a little while. Somehow, and luckily, I eventually remembered.

Actually, I remembered what we have here. What's important, what's not. I'll probably never get to move back to that high place where people can barely go, even now it's expensive beyond the point of ludicrous, but I'd sure like to.

It's quiet, it's near impossible to get to. There's not another human within the sound of pistol fire. The view is incredible.

A better view of myself I've never had.

Travels In The Night

*I*t is a little known fact that I like the dark…dark rooms, dark days and occasionally dark motivations and thoughts. For some reason I seem to think better when the lights are out, the reverse situation to those who are affected with the winter doldrums of Seasonal Affected Disorder. Bright sunlight does little to alter my moods one way or another, however a pitch black night lit only by a shaded moon and a few zillion stars can transport me into a wonderland of imagination unknown during the daylight hours. For one who spends a good deal of their time on the utility-free side of the moon, playing in fantasy worlds born of the quirky lobe of the brain, this is a dandy thing.

Having said that though, and contrary to the beliefs of the few friends who are privy to my troll-like ways, I do not like the dark all the time. Summer camping trips on the banks of a skittering creek, spring-time in the canyon seeking the elusive finned giant, a fall walk during the brief rainbow flash of the leafy color spectrum, those are times when it is good to see the world in technicolor. I can't make up anything quite so nice, proving once again that while fiction reads better, truth is still the stranger and more magnificent of the pair.

Recently, pulling back into the valley after a three week sojourn, I was thankful for the sun. It allowed me to gaze at the mountains. I knew I had made it home.

You see, I just returned from a 4,000 mile jaunt across the country, monster dog and I packed tight in the Jimmy, driving across hill and dale to break bread with family, old friends and sights unseen for a too long number of years. We crossed the moonscapes of Wyoming and the ice blown vastness of the southernmost Dakota. We played on the Devil's Backbone of the Ozarks and were unmercifully mired in the brown Arkansas clay. Only Iowa was a drag. It takes a strong stomach to tolerate screaming Baptist evangelists and 24 hour hog reports on the radio, but then again, occupied territories rarely have unique tourist traps.

We blasted off truck-loads of ammo, talked knives, slurped down mounds of deep fried catfish and determined first hand (on two occasions) what type of terrain is most effective for getting stuck in a four wheel drive. We trimmed the tree, lit the lights, opened the presents and spied upon giant bucks from the forgotten graveyards of Civil War bushwhackers. We spent time with family and wandered the farm in search of childhood treasures. Although the giant cottonwood that had grown around the barbed wire decades before is now gone, victim to lightning and wind and whatever type of Alzheimer's Disease trees are subject to when they near two centuries, the good memories remained. The owls hooted and the coyotes yelped and the icy winter rain poured down.

So it was good. The more things change the more they remain the same. This is especially true of childhood homes. They are always there, and if you are as lucky as I, they always await with open arms. Still, the return to the home of now gives an almost indefinable pleasure.

It was mid-afternoon when I popped back into the valley, a day sunny and cold with clouds puffing around the highest peaks. I rolled down the window to receive a face-full of frigid gale, breathed deep the chill and snowy promise of Montana winter. The dog rose from his nap and began to bounce. I sat a little straighter and began to smile. I rolled into McAllister, said hello to a few friends, and hunkered down with the dog to reset our mental compass. Soon after, the sun made it's daily departure. We were ready.

Under the black quilt of middle evening the two of us sat huddled on the old bench in the back yard, allowing the night to sweep away any lingering concerns or cares.

"Nothing is perfection," I told him, wondering what the many tomorrows would bring. "There are always events to soil the brain, always people to clutter the karma. You strive for that which you desire, keep that which you need, and cast aside that which is useless."

The dark fell full and we sat in silence. Maybe the best part of the deep dark is that it sometimes allows you to see more clearly than at brightest day. When the sun rose the next morning I knew all would be well with the world. Sometimes a place and a moment hit you that way.

"Nothing is perfection," agreed the dog, sniffing the air and uttering a soft woof at a low flying bird…

"But this is close."

Nighttime With A Dog

*B*uffet streaks across the pasture, a brindle colored mass of 150 pound wolfhound puppy whose paws are as of yet too large for his body. Stretching out to unbelievable length as if constructed of rubber, a vision of the full blown giant he will too soon become, this cyclone of a canine loses balance and goes tumbling head over tail in that lopsided, awkward crash particular to oversized young dogs and inebriated old sailors. He couldn't care less, up in a microsecond in search of sticks and rocks and bugs and anything which has reached a sufficient nastiness to invite either a hearty roll or quick consumption. A gourmet this pup is not, which matters little to either him or me.

The Buff is happy with simplicity, living totally for the moment, a trait which we mere mortals should attempt to emulate.

As for myself, leaning against a far tree and enjoying a smoke before the darkness descends completely, I watch my most recent constant companion with a smile. A rolling cloud bank hangs over the canyon, the wind has died down and all is quiet. Somewhere close by a goose lets out a solitary honk. I honk back. The goose is not impressed. No matter, I don't speak goose anyway. I speak dog, or at least I try.

Buffett charges off to contemplate a tall weed. I have to laugh. Of all the wondrous things in creation, dogs must rate near the top of the list. Reveling in his innocent approach to life, recharging my batteries, I wonder what they know that we do not.

That I am a dog person, there is no doubt. Cats are fine, although too aloof for my nature. Horses are ok, but not my cup of tea. Parrots are all right if prepared correctly with the right amount of thyme, lemon juice and rubbed sage. Tropical fish look just dandy in a medical waiting room. Again, I'm no Dr. Doolittle. I only speak dog. Or, at least I try.

Although many have raised eyebrows and shaken their noggins at my close attachments to the four-legged tail-wagging set, I find it quite a pleasant set-up. It is the way it is and should be, for I have always been the solitary sort. Jealous of my privacy, set in my ways, dogs have been a part of my life for as long as I can remember. Few of my romantic interests could handle my eccentricities for long, but the pups just laugh and figure I'm twisted and hang around for the ride. Then they drop a ball in my lap and drag me from the writer's seclusion. No human could get away with that. A dog can do it every time.

As with many of us, I have a family tree of dogs. During childhood it was the beagles, rummaging around on the southern Missouri farm in search of warm spots where deer had slept, or hiking down to my grandmother's hay barn to traverse nations made of straw. Later, it was the venerable black Labrador, that "once in a lifetime if your lucky" kind of dog, as much a part of my life as heart or lungs. We traveled many states together, the Frisbee Master and I, and his passing a couple of years back left a void which will never completely fill. These days, it's the Buffett, a whole new personality of high-octane energy, huge brown eyes and kindly disposition.

All have had their place. All have had their time. All have provided comfort and made me glad to be alive.

It is dark now, the quiet air loud with serenity. I sit on the damp ground and am immediately smothered by a battering ram comprised of giant paws, slobbering tongue and a mind intent on getting it's ears scratched. In this time, in this place, there is nothing else I need. I toss the stick, Buffett chases.

That's how it works. I try to teach him silly tricks. He tries to teach me simplicity. It's a nice arrangement.

He doesn't know it, but I'm getting the good end of the deal.

Long Live The Travelers

I have known many travelers in my time. Some embark on their journeys to escape a bitter past. Others sally forth towards the wild blue in the hope of finding a brighter tomorrow. Some are restless. Some are lost. Some are adventurers. Some simply wish to see the elephant.

A long lost writer friend, Garcia, traveled in the manner of the carnie worker. He lived by his wits, viewing life on the road as a puzzle in intellectual and physical survival. In order to exist, Garcia often displayed a marked lack of conscience. Frankly, I suspect this traveler is dead now, shot by a rampaging husband or knifed by one of the many deranged street folks and dark side characters whose lives he so loved to illustrate with words. Another friend, Sherman, has a bit more class, yet no less wit in his travels. In years past he always managed to find the best and the finest places, from the glitter of Monte Carlo to the sunny beaches of Spain to the spongy bogs of Ireland. He claims to have once woken up on a shrimp boat, a tick-ridden, three legged dog licking his face.

As for self, I joined the ranks of the wanderlusters out of pure confusion. No idea of where to go or what to do, my broken compass has guided me from coast to coast, from the sub-tropical sea shores to the mountains of the Madison Valley, and a place I can finally call home.

We wandering souls are many in number, but the finest traveler of all was Tracy. She achieves this distinction not from her odd and bizarre journey to distant lands, nor even from the things she learned along the way. What makes Tracy special is the way she applies what she learned.

She walked into my Florida office in the mid-80's, a 21 year old kid who wanted to write. Her samples were quite lacking in technical methods, but her style was impeccable. That style, as well as her quiet manner and enthusiasm, convinced me to take her on staff. Watching the rapid progression from fledgling to expert (I think it took about two days) was a pure joy. A few years later, she strolled in and informed me she was leaving.

"Where," I said with downtrodden spirits.

"Here and there," she responded with a grin.

Here and there meant more than I imagined. She criss-crossed the United States before bopping off to Australia. If memory serves, she paid her way in that country by driving dynamite trucks in the gold fields and bartending at some of the roughest bars to be found in the desolate, female starved wilderness of Western Down Under. Scared? Hardly! You do not mess with this petite young thing, for she can cut you down in a flash.

Later, I heard Tracy was serving as first mate on a circumnavigation. I do know she once hiked into the rugged mountains of New Guinea and surreptitiously observed the natives in one tribal ritual or another. She wasn't turned into girl-stew by these near Stone Age primitives, which I found amazingly lucky.

About five years passed without word until, during one of my many escapes from somewhere to somewhere, a curious urge led me toward Tracy's former Arkansas town and a quick check of the phone books. Surprisingly, she had come home. The call was made, and my little red sports car struggled up the hill to her house, a much over-loaded U-Haul tow-trailer threatening to stall me out on the steep grades bordering her Boston Mountain nest. I only wanted to give a quick hello, share a few nostalgic minutes, and then back on the road. Of course, she would not allow this.

Tracy wined me and dined me, gave me laughter and succor and nourishment of the soul. Trust me, in those days this soul needed all the nourishment it could get, and I passively (eagerly) accepted her gracious hospitality with concealed cartwheels. The only problem arose when she refused to take a cent for her trouble and expense.

We almost argued about this, until she explained in her quiet voice a reason which was undeniably pure, and which has remained with me to this day.

You see, in her travels around the globe, Tracy had slept in barns, stalls and the homes of kind strangers who remained strangers for but a moment. She had been given help and kindness and support by her fellow man, and she felt she owed a debt to the world for this blessing. She would not let me contribute a dime toward our merry making. She felt that hospitality and kindness are something to be shared freely, passed along without thought or hesitation. All she asked was that, whenever possible, I do the same for another.

I do not know where Tracy is right now, but since we run into each other every seven or eight years, it doesn't matter. The bold/shy young girl who grew into a bold/stunning young woman, the mousey little thing who simply wanted to write stories, imparted a message more eloquent than the finest novel, more beautiful than the brushstrokes of a post-modern Leonardo.

She taught me that we are all travelers, no matter whether we stray afar or remain in the towns of our birth. Every greeting, every smile, every encounter with a new face, tree, bird, what-have-you is but another journey. The miles matter not. It's how we welcome the traveler that counts.

I am not as selfless as Tracy, not nearly as giving, wise or kind. Not even close. Most of the time I'm too self possessed to emulate her wisdom in greeting life, her insight in dealing with her fellow humans. Still, her ways give me hope for the human race, so I try to keep them in mind.

In these times of rapid change and mindless turmoil, so should we all.

Bigger Than Life

When the phone call came, I figured that Burgeson had been killed in a plane wreck. He was not the type of guy who should have been a pilot, let alone the stick man of a little puddle jumper like a Cessna 150. Burgie, for being a jock, was a bit accident prone. He also had a tendency to forget stuff, like where he'd left his contact lenses. Not a good thing to do if you're a pilot.

But, Burgie wasn't killed in a plane wreck. It was a freak accident down in the Land of Mormon that got him, if you want to know, and another reason I've never been fond of Utah. The young man who looked like an Olympic alternate on the Norwegian wrestling team was building electrical transmission towers through the Rockies, had climbed 120 some odd feet to the top of one on a routine check of bolt torque, and the whole damn thing collapsed under him. We later found out it was a billion to one shot. Somehow a bunch of metal fatigued bolts had ended up in a shipment of construction supplies. Somehow, they all landed in one tower. Somehow, they gave way right when Burgie hit maximum altitude. End of story. Another friend snagged away before his time.

Still though, the accident that took him young a decade ago is really not the subject of this story. The subject is how to live well, and I can think of no better example.

Burgeson was one of those guys that was kind to kids and animals and old ladies. He had a strong moral character, possibly the result of his upbringing, and had a certain innocent approach to life that contradicted his intelligence. He had a deaf brother, and I've always wondered if Burg was one of those people who truly counted their blessings for being healthy and whole. He seemed to occasionally pop up with voluptuous girlfriends, initially drawn in by his Nordic good looks, who then fell madly in love and hung around in hopes of getting a husband. He never worried about us trying to snag them away, for to attempt such a thing would have bothered even our shady sensibilities.

Once, while working for a Kansas City engineering firm during a summer off from college, Burgie sight unseen accepted a rental apartment in one of K.C.'s worst ghettos. To the north, if I recall, lived a cut-rate mortician who had been stacking bodies in the basement and burying empty boxes for the last 15 years. To the south was red-light house whose hand painted sign advertised "Indian Herb Baths." We told Burgie there was an old Indian named Herb who lived there, and it was probably best to not consider deeply the goings on behind the battered door. Street prophets were common, as were rotund and aged hookers, as were good jazz places we wouldn't step foot in for fear of mutilation and/or terminal wounds. Gunshots and sirens and screams in the night were rivaled only by the roaches in terms of prevalence.

Anybody else would have been shot within five minutes in that part of town, at least anybody who looked as if they just immigrated from Norway, but not Burgie. The locals took to him right off, and I recall him mentioning hanging out in the local barber shop and jawing with the neighbors. He enjoyed life, looked forward to the future with such intensity that the feeling seemed to spill out of his pores and take hold of those in close proximity. The sense of humor was infectious, he could be as wild as the rest of us, but he had a conscience. The stories are endless. I won't bother you with them further.

The funeral sucked rocks. It is not just the good who die young, but when they do, you notice it more. A whole crew of us caravaned up to northern Wisconsin and I remember my friend Ed and I having to leave the visitation before he got too pissed at the saccharine sweet, ice cream suited parlor director and popped him in the nose. Funerals in America, lets face it, are rarely fun. They celebrate death, rather than life, and such is not appropriate for one who truly knew how to live.

Life goes on, and the years pass quickly. Too quickly, I think. Burgie had been out of mind for some time, until a few weeks ago when I received a letter from an old flame. She's married now, was wishing me well in Montana, and imparted the closing advice that one should live life to the fullest, enjoying every second.

I thought about that, thought about a long gone friend, and decided the flame of the past was only partially right. Life is a grand thing, but when living in a place bigger than life, the words take on entirely different dimensions. Burgeson knew that internally, didn't need the outside influence. I'm the opposite. I require the constant reassurance of 10,000 foot peaks and raging windstorms and 150 pound dogs to drive the message home. Cynical hermit writer that I am, I need magnificence to make me awestruck. I need "bigger than life" to put my life in perspective.

So, I went outdoors and drew deep a breath of mountain air, remembered the whitetail doe I had tripped across the morning before, and watched in quiet reverence as the setting sun set the sky ablaze. Quit concerning yourself with the trivial, I told myself, don't worry about the quest for fortune and glory. You have found fortune in an eagle's cry and a rushing river, and though you may not obtain glory, you are surrounded by the glorious.

I threw a salute to the setting sun, more brilliant today than yesterday, somewhat smaller than tomorrow.

To Soar On Dreams

My Dad and I built Hang Loose in the north end of our barn when I was 12 or 13 years old. She was a 15.5' long Chanute-style biplane hang glider with a 27' wingspan and 4.5' chord. A great looking craft chock full of many wires and struts, the intrepid pilot would hang in the middle of the glider by his armpits, turning and banking by weight control alone.

I wanted to fly, my Dad wanted to see me fly. I always thought that was cool, for most parents would start whining about broken legs and medical bills should their weird kid decide he wants to make like the Bird-Man of the Andes. Actually, he probably figured that if we didn't build the damn thing I would jump off the house with a parachute made out of bed sheets. I was a stubborn kid, and a little odd even back then. Some things never change.

Completely undaunted by the lack of decent flying hills on our southwest Missouri farm, we spent countless hours tightening wires and shaping struts and attempting to construct a decent air-foil surface. A couple of hours driving time would get you into the deeper Ozarks, where there were many hills of adequate size for take-off, but they were all covered with trees, brush, moonshiners and canoe rental joints. No matter, there was more to this voyage than mere air time. I studied up on coefficients of lift and dihedrals and glide angles, he got stuck repairing all the stuff I screwed up. Call it a symbiotic relationship, if you will. I'll call it a good Dad's dedication and caring.

We finished the Hang Loose after a couple hundred hours of delicate work. She was a beauty, a polyethylene covered bi-plane which would have brought tears to the eyes of Orville and Wilbur. Unfortunately, she never flew.

Truth be known, Hang Loose only got off the ground once, and that was when a doozie of a wind storm picked her up and sent her sailing smack into our machine shed. We left her there for a while, up-ended, tail section staring down from 15 feet in the air. The problem was in our design. The bamboo which the plans specified for the frame was not indigenous to Missouri, so we were forced to make do with light plywood. Plywood is indigenous to everywhere, but, and here's a tip, it does not serve well on the design of a lighter than air machine.

No matter, I flew Hang Loose a million times in my mind. Imagination is not governed by such silly physical things as gravity and wing loading.

That was nearly 30 years ago. Other interests took over from flying. I think we eventually got tired of dodging the old Hang Loose's battered carcass and hauled her down to the ditch. I wandered here and there and yon over the next two decades, ostensibly in search of the eternal something, but in all honesty remaining predominately Earth-bound myself. Finally, I experienced my own doozie of a storm, which luckily blew me into the Madison Valley, home of eagles and fine people and other creatures that soar on magnificent wings of grace and kindness.

Here, high up in the sky, I no longer care deeply about the technicalities of life. I can fly every day without leaving my back yard, a lesson which I think my Dad was trying to impart those long years ago in the north end of our barn. It's the simple things that count, the floating hued rainbows and fresh blossomed flowers and new born ponies that romp in the fields.

One should test their wings. One should sail to the clouds. Adventure is the stuff of magic, but the happiness of home and friends brings equal reward. Success is measured in many ways, and perhaps the best way is through the joy of the journey, treasuring our brief moments on this planet for their own sake.

One does not need wings to take to the sky. One needs only the desire. One needs only to hang loose.

The Lesson

*T*he woods on my grandmother's farm are called Prosperity, named by my maternal grandfather and noted for its pretty stands of cedar and near surface veins of coal. As a kid, they seemed to me somehow possessed, a place of mystery and personality and wonder. Friendly, yet proud. Aloof, yet inviting. They beckoned to a part of the soul which believed in magic.

Inside Prosperity one finds a temperamental creek surrounded by near impenetrable brush, deadfalls and the occasional blackberry bush. The beagles and I traipsed through there on many occasions, for the beagles and I were notorious traipsers. The beagles are buried there, as is a collie, as are memories, as was a lesson I almost never learned.

I think of Prosperity more often these days than in years past, for there was a period of life when the magic seemed to have died. Those years were fraught with danger and confusion and a pace of life which, miraculously, did not inflict permanent damage. Back then, worry seemed not just the rule, but indeed the badge of honor. There was the day to day grind, the stress, the foolish attempts to live up to the expectations set by others rather than the fulfillment of necessities asked by self. When things were bad, I fretted and stewed, joining fellow ulcer candidates in self indulgent praises to the gods of solicitude. When things were good, I worried over the fact that I had nothing over which to worry.

When the change came, I do not know. It was slow and gradual and only shed it's cloak one sleeve at a time. There is a silent and all wise portion of the head which seems to know when it's time to softly tap the brake pedal. Suddenly, I found myself caring less than ever before, and ironically, caring more. I cared less about the things that once seemed big, for those items had lost their worth. I cared more about the things that once seemed small, for they became priceless.

A mountain sunrise took precedence over an employer's implied harangue. The frantic antics of a playful pup superseded respectability and the opinions of others. The sunrises and the pups and the creeks and the laughter would not now be traded for gold or diamonds or acclaim. Money? It will come and it will go. Success? That depends upon your definition.

It became apparent, this simplest, yet most elusive fact in the world. I suddenly understood that we are on this planet but for a blink, and to waste even a second is both stupid and selfish. One does not look at a painting to analyze the brush strokes. One looks for an appreciation of beauty, a sense of awe. So it is with art. So it is, or at least should be, with life.

I see new friends, share in their tales and marvel that it should be so good. I wake to the sound of geese and cranes, an overly affectionate, over-sized pup lapping my face and staring down with quizzical brown eyes. Each morning I stare at the mountains. Each morning I am amazed.

The woods on my grandmother's farm are called Prosperity, named by my maternal grandfather and noted for its pretty stands of cedar and near surface veins of coal. They stand now as they stood then. A place of mystery and personality and wonder. I see them, not with eyes, but with the clarity of newfound respect. Solemn, yet seductive, reverent, yet playful, they beckon to a part of the soul which knows that loosening the grip improves the grasp. Prosperity is the best part of me, the part which realizes that time is too valuable to rush.

Prosperity is there. Prosperity is here. It knows no borders and will follow wherever, and whenever, you allow.

The beagles live there, as does a collie, as do memories, as does a lesson I finally learned.

Reunion

*T*hey tracked me down, I'm not sure how, just a couple of days ago. These were people I've seen maybe twice in 15 years, good friends from the olden times. I like these folks, for our conversations do not feel particularly strained, despite all the time and distance. Old friends, those with whom you've broken contact as your respective roads forked in opposite directions, are often the most difficult people to speak with. After the updates on kids and jobs and new cities, after the nostalgia talk is completed, (that can be embarrassing if some of your personal nostalgia is better left in the past) a cloud of uncomfortable silence settles down like pea soup fog in London.

There are only a handful of old friends with whom I've kept in constant touch, people who know my present life and allow me into theirs. There are even fewer who can ring up every 15 years and not make the conversation feel forced. These guys fit the latter category, thank God. It was good to hear from them, but I could tell that we had few things in common save our history.

They were inviting me to a reunion, and as with most such events involving groups and social interaction, I politely declined. That unsettling silence which takes place after the pre-ordained reunion pleasantries makes me itch and sneeze and turn either scarlet or tail, whichever comes first. Seeing people you once knew, but with whom you are no longer acquainted, always makes me flash back to the nightmares of a junior high dance, guys lined up on one side, smacking each other on the arm, girls on the other, tittering about the latest teen heart throb/bubble gum rock star to grace the cover of Tiger Beat.

Some people like such stuff, so maybe this is merely idiosyncrasy on my part. Personal questions coming from familiar faced strangers are vexing, and oftentimes require polite lies. For one whose life has been a little less than traditional, the queries are predictable. "You never got married?" "You never settled down?" "Dating anyone?" Those inquiries are consistent, and I've never been sure quite how to answer. How do you explain that it is the fate of the die-hard romantic to be lacking in romantic success? How do you explain that the overly emotional must always keep a tight rein on their emotions, least they over-ride brain and common sense and result in unsightly explosions of passion and anger, a stew of honey and thorns, which without constant attention, boils over the edge of the kettle?

You try and explain these things honestly, become flushed and flustered, give up, and hit the punch bowl, hoping it is spiked with something other than ginger ale.

"You look the same," they say, which is only a slight lie as I was much more gray at age 21 than I am now, but just as long haired, just as moody, just as prone to the writer's extreme changes of internal climate, just as much of a control freak in the past tense as in the present. "You haven't changed," they say, which always flares a match and sends me scurrying for the coat closet and the latest pay-for-view at the Holiday Inn. "You just didn't look," I think.

To discuss one's life in fleeting manner with old friends might be pleasant. A five minute phone call could probably do it, sate the curiosity of "whatever happened to Billy Bob?" But, these two or three day affairs more often than not turn into some sort of competition. Life shouldn't be about competition, boasts of acquisition, or the comparison shopping over success and failure so common on the American Joyride.

Many of my friends opted for the white picket fence. As long as it makes them happy, that's wonderful. I opted to fence with white pickets. Such is life. Many of the old friends, not all, but many, are entirely different personalities than the folks I once knew, and that's a good thing. Some have integrated past and present and we can communicate freely. That's a better thing. Others look to the future, and while they are the most rare, they are also the ones I most cherish and with whom I speak often.

No, I don't think I need a reunion. I have my friends, both old and new, which is much more satisfying than a regurgitation of the past. We all changed, for better or worse. We all took the paths commanded by either fate or choice or both. Like all humans, we have our foibles and follies and triumphs and failures.

I came to live in the mountains, to move away, as much as possible, from the things of man. I came here to write and tell stories. I came to escape the past and discover the future. I came for the rich fullness of life and the peaceful emptiness of solitude.

I came to a long forgotten home which I'd never before seen.

Such is reunion enough.

The Crow

*J*ames Rufus Crow was born in Columbia, Missouri on or about January 28th, 1979. He was on death row when we met, a mere 24 hours from being put down by lethal injection. He was big and black, at first glance fearsome in appearance, the type of guy you would never want to meet in a dark alley. Such fears were ill founded, for although he would hurt a flea, most other living beings were quite safe in his presence.

James Rufus Crow had one of the best souls I've ever met, and luckily, I had the power to grant pardon from the executioner's needle. I did, and the next 13 odd years were filled with a never ending series of daily misadventures, conversation and downright weirdness.

James Rufus Crow, you see, was a dog. He was my dog and this is his birthday. The thought of his passing is still like a sword through my gut.

I can rarely think of that animal without breaking down. It's not that I'm unthankful for the years we shared, for I would not trade them for all the riches in the world. It's not that I do not remember our every trek through numerous forests, swims on the lake or exploration of water filled caves. The constant good times are burned into my mind, heart and soul. It's not that I fail to cherish the miles we covered, traveling together through something like 10 different states in a whole series of Camaros, Trans Ams, Rancheros and Monte Carlos. It's just that I miss him.

People come and go, and loneliness has never been a trait to which I'm susceptible. I like solitude. In all my life, I can honestly say I've been lonely but once. You have to understand, I loved my dog.

You will laugh at this, but Crow spoke English. There was no command one could give to which he would not respond. I figured out one time he officially understood over 100 different requests. Unofficially, I suspect he spoke 17 languages and 432 dialects. One time, in jest, I told him to find my lost cigarette lighter. Five minutes later it was lying between his paws. Many times, something else you need not believe, I did not even have to speak. He knew what I was thinking before I did. It was bizarre. It was wonderful.

I'm recalling all this, telling you, because James Rufus Crow is more than a memory. An old photograph, taken when I was young and unscarred by either life or more physical things, is propped on my dresser. A young man sits on a rock outcrop in a deep forest, his arm lovingly encircles a younger, and much beloved partner in adventure. A lock of hair sits within that framed memory. Guess who?

And somehow, I still feel him around the house. Buffett, my dog now, is a great little 170 pound monster and my feelings for him are deep. We have much fun, but there simply cannot be another Crow. I wouldn't want there to be. I did not acquire my little Wolfhound for replacement value. We joined up, much like my coming to the mountains, to begin anew.

It took me some time to realize that James Rufus Crow is gone only in body. It was a long haul from mindless grief to observing him in the waterfalls and shooting stars and night blast lightning. He's gone. He's here.

But, I do miss him, his laughter, the unbridled life he brought into my life. It was two years ago today that I held him in my arms for the final time, watched his eyes close and heard his last breath. I lost it for a while back then, and wondered this past week why I'd been in such a horrible and foul mood, totally unfit for human interaction. Then I remembered the day.

I can still see him launching his 120 pounds of massive labrador muscle through the air, a giant, midnight flying squirrel hot on the trail of a 163 gram Frisbee. He would swim upstream against the never yielding current of the Missouri River, the sheer power of nature clashing head on with the sheer will of an obstinate and unbeatable dog. Strange that I ended up so close to the headwaters of that coursing waterway, the torrent which he viewed as a playful adversary.

Perhaps Crow knew something that I did not. Perhaps he was heading this direction long before the notion was a twinkle in my brain. Perhaps, and this wouldn't have been unusual, he was trying to show me the way.

Perhaps, as in the old days, he's just been waiting for me to catch up.

Adios. Hasta la vista. Hello old friend.

Christmas Spirits

*B*uffett the wolfhound was in high fever. Whether he was bored, frisky or just in a malevolent mood was and is yet to be determined. All I know is that he had managed to create one Gawd-Awful mess on the living room floor, one for which I strongly doubted he would wax apologetic and offer to run get the Dust Buster.

The shreds of paper were everywhere, tiny things, millions of bits of some long dead deciduous tree scattered from here to yon to Cleveland. How a six foot dog that prefers fetching eight foot limbs had the patience to make like Ollie North's paper shredder, carefully ripping the newspaper circular into one inch strips, I'll never understand. He usually doesn't notice anything under 40 pounds. All I could tell is that something was under the boy's skin, and I'm fairly certain it wasn't fleas, seborrhea or even the heartbreak of psoriasis.

On hands and knees I began to Hoover up the damage, noticing a piece of paper which was still relatively intact. The circular, it seems, was from one of those nameless Mart-Marts where prices are always low and the canned Christmas carols buzz incessantly through your occipital lobe in manner similar to a high speed Black and Decker crossed with a Chinese Water Torture device. Those stores are evil; I swear they are loaded with hypnotic gas and subliminal messages which force one to purchase worthless trinkets and faulty doo-dads and the uncolorized version of How The Grinch Stole A Wonderful Life.

Buff sat on the couch, laughing I think, and wondering if I got it. He's not the subtle type when it comes to delivering messages. Then again, when dealing with one who's allowed themselves to be hemmed in by the holiday fog of hype and consumption, something stronger than a quiet word and a tap on the shoulder is required.

My buddy Ransom Jack says that this time of year is loaded with tons of guilt and debt and depression. He's right, and that's a shame. Most people are so heavily infected with the rabid buying frenzy, frantically scribbling out scores of jolly cards, racing from town to town and from store to store, wondering if they spent too much, fearful that they spent too little, that they forget why they're out spending and scribbling in the first place. It's a remake of Death Race 2000 on a one horse open sleigh. Hand over that Mighty Morphine Power Ranger or I'll make your day.

People admit tax time makes them sweat blood, but since they don't want the neighbors to think they are the Ebeneezer type, they smile and chortle and chuckle during the holidays, all the while developing a shopping derived duodenal ulcer. Their insides twist and warp as if they are the fourth actor in a Three Scrooges short, while outwardly they give a hearty smile and drop some pocket change in the Salivation Army bucket, as if you could ignore those bell ringers without feeling you are a major jerk whose immortal soul is going to be stir-fried in the eternal barbecue for not parting with a handful of Roosevelt dimes.

Again, it's a shame. The tense shoulders, aching skull, churning stomach and frequent checking of the credit limit are not what it's all about, no matter what the talking heads on the boob tube tell you. Ignore their statistics of the financial ups and downs of the buying season, for they're not important. It's about something else entirely, an internal feeling which I guaran-damn-tee you won't find amidst the network vidiot pap.

Forget the religious aspect for a minute. Although that's what Christmas is based upon, and something more often than not conveniently overlooked, this time of year has the ability to give something else, if you'll but let it. Underlying all the hustle, bustle and muscle there is a core of calmness, an opportunity to make nice with self and others. The Christmas spirit does not require that you worship in a certain way or act in a certain prescribed manner, that's entirely optional. What it can do is allow the chance to maybe heal some old wounds, both to self and others. It does allow the ability to perpetrate acts of simple kindness, either openly or in anonymity, to both total strangers and close friends. The season of giving, as it's commonly called, entails giving more of yourself than it does anything else, or at least it should. There is the possibility for happy nostalgia, thoughts of those far away, a friendly word and maybe even intrinsic remorse for things long gone. It is a time to give, but only if you feel strongly about it. Giving for the feeling which arises deep in the gut, not because of the expectations of society or the guilt complex brought on by the cascading ad campaigns. It is more a time to think well than to purchase wisely.

Of course, some will say that these opportunities exist all year long. That may be true in a ideal world, but since the ideal world has yet to be manufactured, the statement is merely wishful thinking by second stringers on the dream team. Something about Christmas, and the birth of the New Year, creates the atmosphere of reflection and bandaged soul with which we can build something greater than what went before. We are permitted to attempt a fix-it job on things which have been scarred or broken, even if the repair remains forever within our own psyche.

Such concepts and desires cannot be purchased with an American Express during a blue light special. They can only be grasped freely, given with true expression and received joyfully as your heart allows.

I sucked up the last of the Wolfhound's Mass Mail Mart Massacre and dumped it in the trash, along, hopefully, with some other leaking garbage I'd been lugging about for much too long. Laughing at my thick skull, Buffett gave three short barks.

Strange dog, the Buff. His belly shook like a bowl full of jelly.

Love Me...Love My Dog

My dog is bigger than some European countries, kinder than most people, and has a tendency to sleep something like 12 hours out of every day. He is stubborn, usually smells like river scum, and (I hope he doesn't read this) is not terribly bright. Buffett is a fun companion to have around, friendly as all get out, but he will never have a Nobel Prize sitting on the doghouse mantle.

My dog is a little set in his ways, does what he wants when he wants, and cast dispersions upon the character of those who either cause unneeded stress or prevent his immediate gratification. He hates crowds and cities. He needs tranquilizers to drive in heavy traffic. His diet tends heavily toward the meat family, and being Irish, he is partial to ale and single malts. He is never happier than when running around in the boonies, not a soul in sight, checking out splashing creeks and summer snowbanks and things that go bump in the day.

Buffett's world is not a democracy, and that's how it should be. His needs are simple, and those who would occasionally attempt to alter them (IE: me) are simply sticking their nose where it doesn't belong and asking to get it tweaked.

I have the sneaking suspicion that most people would find Buffett highly obnoxious after a very short time period. I also have the sneaking suspicion that Buffett couldn't care less.

My dog and I have a lot in common.

I like to sleep about 12 hours a day, although I usually only get five, and am also stubborn and hairy. I've been accused of smelling a tad gamey, and absolutely despise traffic, crowds and cities. Although I'm Scottish rather than Irish, I eat meat, drink ale and am never happier than when making like the Mad Hermit of the Madison. I try and be nice to people, listen to their advice, but will generally engage my own convoluted strategy regardless of what was said or by whom. My needs are simple, and folks who wish to complicate them are cruisin' for a nose tweak.

I only believe in democracy when I'm the sole registered voter. That's an independent stance, granted, but considering the upcoming holiday it's quite an appropriate topic.

I see many of our freedoms being leached away. They aren't being stolen by some evil Big Brother, and they aren't being legislated out of existence. Our freedoms are evaporating because many of us are selling out our sense of independence. Income too often wins out over integrity, status too often gains more respect than sincerity. Money can buy a certain level of happiness, whoever claimed otherwise was just sour grapes, but it can't buy character.

A lot of folks are trying to do just that, and they may even think they're getting away with it. We ignore these individuals' lack of personal substance (Nice clothes the emperor's got, huh Ma?) because of their big cars, big houses, big flyrods and $50,000 per acre hunks of scrub brush. We don't call things as they are because we benefit financially. In short, we sell out to the almighty buck, and in doing so, give away majority ownership in the intestinal fortitude and rugged independence that built this place to begin with.

In the fire sale of the soul, self respect is the first thing to go. After that's depleted, when the independent nature is given away, the grasping of additional freedoms is an easy task.

Don't misunderstand…I'm all for newcomers and visitors and I'm all for making money. I've just never understood folks who think their wealth makes them impressive. A designer jockstrap or big inheritance from grandpa's truss empire does not give a person carte blanche to trash the place. As long as one recognizes that Prince and Pauper will be judged on character rather than cash flow, realize they will not gain deferential treatment due to an inflamed wallet size, there's no problem.

Rich or poor, people who don't respect this place have no business being here. They shouldn't be tolerated in general, let alone be catered to. Then again, I'm a lot like my dog and our needs are simple. We just like looking at the mountains and splashing through the streams and doing what we damn well please without some Yahoo getting in our face or trying to impress us with their importance. We go where we want and do what we want and don't owe a soul (except maybe ourselves) a single, solitary thing. We like the independent life, and even though we may smell funny, we are happy with that life no matter the locale.

I've seen independence traded for baubles and beads before—that's probably why I've moved a lot—and hope to never see it again. Trust me, the cost is astronomically high.

Sunrises and eagles and things of that nature don't cost a red cent, and yet they are priceless. Independence and freedom cannot be purchased or stolen, but they can be given away.

We already have wealth beyond compare... what the hell more could we want?

Clark

"There are three essences to life," he told me. "You have to have something to believe in. You have to have something to look forward to. You have to have something to love."

Clark told me that a couple weeks ago, right after the diagnosis came in. He lived by those good rules until yesterday morning. Clark died at 4:00 a.m. He would be 62 today.

Clark Johnson was a big Irishman, a Vermonter who had come to McAllister a few years back because he didn't feel ready for a rocking chair. He was brutally blunt, but would not intentionally hurt a fly. He was a classic hunter, but sometimes he just liked to sit hidden in the woods with his bow and watch the whitetails, not even taking the readily available shot. He was strong as an ox, but would burst into tears during discussions of his hero, Abraham Lincoln. He could out-fight, out-cuss, out-fish, out-hunt, out-work anybody I've ever met, all while discussing the philosophy of human nature or quoting Shakespeare.

Clark was my neighbor and landlord. He was my fishing buddy. Most of all, he was my friend.

Clark grew up in various orphanages. He once told me that the first roof over his head was called "the home for little wanderers." By the time he was 10 he had figured out how to earn money and live off the land. That was the year, he said, when he ran away from the orphanage. He got 200 miles before being turned in by a well meaning, but misguided adult. Clark ran away a lot after that, and though he'd usually get caught, though they'd usually beat him, it didn't break his spirit.

Clark eventually found a home in the Air Force. He was big for his age, and the recruiters never even guessed that he was only 14 years old. Clark liked it. He said few things were better than a bed, warm clothes and all the food you could eat.

I can't tell you too many of the stories about Clark in this venue, for too many people would freak out. He was a wild man. I can tell you that he once hitchhiked from Vermont to Seattle via Mexico. I can tell you that he must have cut a mean figure in the 50's, clad in black leather and riding 'round the country on his Harley. I can tell you he was kind to dogs, fed wild birds and rabbits, ate rattlesnake and was hell on wheels when angry. I can tell you one day he walked in after performing a Robin Hood maneuver, perfectly splitting an arrow at 50 yards, and the smile was that of a kid.

Clark loved jokes and he loved life. He was a voracious reader, and was consistently amused by plot lines involving people who would whine over their petty problems. Clark knew how hard life could be, but every blow only made him happier, more resilient, more joyous to be healthy and strong. When life hit him hard, he hit back harder, all claws and fists and brains. Clark usually won.

But finally he started coughing and he went to the doctor and she said he didn't have long but before the cancer could get him something broke in his head and he was done. I don't want to talk about that part. It was quick, and that's pretty much how Clark wanted it, and it wouldn't surprise me if the son of a gun planned it that way.

So now there's a big hole in my life. It's the same hole that is there for all of us who knew him, no matter if we were acquainted only briefly or for decades. Clark taught us all many things. Mostly, he taught us that simplicity is beautiful, that kindness is priceless. He taught us how good it is to live.

"As of right now, there are no closed seasons and no limits." That's what Clark said to his friend Tim on the first fishing trip after they found the cancer. I like that. It fits.

One of these days we'll all take him up to the Yaak Valley, the place he had chosen to rest, and scatter his ashes to the breeze. On that day I'll remember Clark, and behind the tears will be the happiness of having known a man who truly understood how life works.

Cast long and shoot straight, Clark Johnson. We'll see you in the rivers. We'll hear you in the wind.

You gave us something to believe in, something to look forward to and something to love. You made life a little better.

A better gift, or a better friend, I cannot imagine.

The Fox and The Hound

*T*he Mama fox raced across the pasture, an orange flash backlit by the fading red barn and dying rays of an amber sunset. She spied me and ground to a halt. An onlooker, an interloper in her private domain, I felt a quizzical glance as she plopped up on her haunches and gave me the once over. Actually, truth be known, it was more like a twice over, or maybe a three times over, for we engaged in a five minute stare down. Mama fox won in this battle of wills and curiosity, of course, darting for cover as soon as I advanced a few steps her way for a closer view. She'd seen enough. She was bored with the process.

Buffett the Wolfhound was oblivious, youngster that he is, engaged in his own mental battle with a tall weed and the sound of a sandhill down in the slew. He has a short attention span, the Buffett dog, more inclined to food and people and anything taller than his 34" at the shoulder height. Buff may be smarter than I, for he knew the fox was both as transitory and permanent as the night. He bounced and laughed and chased imaginary jackrabbits, never once considering anything but the moment's notice, if that. I stood there and stared at Mama fox. Hell, I just thought she was pretty.

She was…but then again, the giant little canine hit the nail at least partially on the head. He nipped at my sleeves and growled at my shoelaces as I stood in silence, afraid of shattering the moment. The Buff didn't care. "Let's play, Boss," he said in his seal-like bark, huge brown eyes staring up full of mischief and unhatched plans. "Lets rock. Places to go. People to see."

When do you go forward? When do you step back? What route is more important? Which is more fun? Dogs know this stuff, but unfortunately, people don't. There's a reason for that. People have a nasty tendency to establish parameters and formulate plans and contemplate the future before the present makes itself evident. They regurgitate the past in the same manner that the monster pup shakes and tears at his well chawed knuckle bone. Sad, that is, for it makes us miss much and cause each other much sorrow. Viewing each moment as a new beginning is a trait which, I conjecture, most of we mere mortals are incapable. Maybe it's because we have thumbs or something, the ability to grasp things. We grasp too many things, inevitable vise-grip graspers that we are, most of which are imaginary at best and paranoid at worst. We desire to hold onto each moment too long, afraid that another wondrous sight may never come again. We seek reason where there is only emotion, search for clues in a mystery that is blatantly obvious. We do not believe in magic. We doubt our own instincts. We cannot rid ourselves of ancient baggage, have not the force of will to toss the soiled and unwanted Samsonite off the precipice.

Dogs know better; great things come when you believe all things are great. Love comes when one's heart is open to love. When viewed from that perspective, all time, each butterfly and every flower and every kind word is a treasure.

But as I said, being one of those aforementioned mere mortals, and for certain filled with more human frailties and insecurities than most, I felt a tinge of sadness as the Mama fox raced out of view. Luckily the feeling only lasted a minute, for the giant little Wolfhound did not allow me to contemplate the loss of something wild and free and beautiful. One more time, he nipped at the sleeves and growled at the shoelaces and tore the pasture asunder as he circled me at full tilt with the rapture for life that only a giant little Wolfhound can feel.

I played the game until he was bored, watching as he sped off to investigate other sights of awe, stuff like waving limbs and low flying nighthawks and more tall weeds, knowing all too well that soon I would once again worry over a loss that had not occurred, fearing the future nearly as much as I dreamed of the future's potential.

I wondered if I would ever see the Mama fox again, would she grace me with her presence, would we ever stare into each other's eyes, nature and civilization crossing paths in mutual wonder?

Fear, ambivalence, avoidance…these things are the death of the human spirit and the rust which eats away at the foundation of risk and unborn accomplishment. To not seek, to not try, is a fate worse than all else. I think (though can seldom live up to the fact) that in order to truly live one must hope and believe in miracles.

The next night the fox returned.

The hound looked at me with his big brown eyes.

"Of course," he said.

Jungle Drums

*T*he jungle drums begin in the murky stillness before the new dawn, their rhythm born not of screaming jaguars, chittering simians or painted natives whacking a hollow log, but rather arising from the poignant song of sandhill, coyote and songbird. The primordial mating tunes ring true in either case, purity of nature is a constant this time of year, but it is the latter crew which brings me a sense of peace and understanding. It is more familiar. It is the sound of home.

The conductor waves his magic wand and the jungle drums tap out their lyrical cadence. They awaken me from a deep slumber, building ever louder to a sustained crescendo of 1,000 myriad voices, a Gregorian chorus of fur, feather and whistling winds. Listen long enough and you will travel to a far place, that part of man which was buried long ago in the quest for quick, easy and convenient. Luckily, though that wilder, more innocent part of the soul may lie under miles of modern day rubble, it does survive, smoldering in wait for moments such as this.

The conductor lays a single brushstroke against the violet sky, a canvas hanging heavy as wet velvet, and a jagged streak of red fire lights the albino peaks. The jungle drums continue, nature's symphony meeting the original laser light show. I watch and I listen. I feel as a mote of dust in a Kansas cyclone. My priorities suddenly seem tiny.

Though I will no doubt forget the lesson as the sun climbs high into the sky, for those fleeting minutes I know what is real.

It is the curse of man that he rarely feels too deeply or for too long. We are a mentally transient species, our brains turning corners and making leaps in a metabolic frenzy rivaling either a Pratt and Whitney engine or an extremely ravenous hummingbird. Our thought processes flit always to the next flagrant flower, the next beckoning color, before the digestion process barely has a chance to take nourishment from the first. We run towards the light. We flee from the dark. We seek truth and beauty, and in our arrogance, think that such things can be purchased or controlled.

I have often been more guilty of this trait than most. Although there is nothing wrong with wondering what's over the next hill, nothing inherently bad in feeling compelled to see the elephant, the image of greener pastures has consistently lured me from things fine and good before I realized their inestimable worth. The next pretty face might be prettier. The next mountain might be higher. The next ocean might be wider. The search is a good thing, it is one of the aspects of man that leads me to believe he might survive, but failing to fully appreciate the journey is a crime against self.

This offense against obvious gifts seems to be occurring with increasing frequency these days. We are more concerned with social posturing than with quiet enjoyment. We buy our pleasures to impress others. We devastate and over-populate the pristine environment with our desire to escape, forgetting that the urge to flee stems from our destruction of the last place we settled. We build and doze and cut, and then point out to all that will listen of our comradeship with nature.

Recently, I told a friend that my fondest desire was to move far to the back country, somehow live beyond the reach of power companies and designer labels and the country club mind-sets of folks with too much cash and not enough sense. A hunk of land, a little cabin, many pups, maybe a couple solar panels to run the pump and the typewriter, a wall of dog-eared books, and definitely a good woodstove. He agreed, intimating that 21st century technology and a 19th century lifestyle would beat most of the nonsense that blares from the papers and electronic noise box.

Hardships abound in such a scenario, creature comforts would largely consist of hanging out with creatures. Some might find such a desire foolish, naive and maybe even a tad misanthropic. It is none of those. Peace is defined in different ways for different people. Mine comes from solitude, from surprise acts of human kindness, from a hundred other things.

Perhaps, in retrospect, it is cynical to hold that man cannot care too deeply or for too long. Perhaps, like that wild part of the soul which shows itself in the pre-dawn still, our ability to revere the pure and simple merely lies dormant. Perhaps, it would fully waken if we but allowed it.

Of course, I'll no doubt forget all this, even if only temporarily, while lummoxing around through the daily duties. Maybe that's how it's supposed to be. Maybe, because they are valuable, our ability to remember the joy of precious moments is but the test of our worthiness to receive them. If such is true, I will try and hold tightly to that which is real, and try and set free that which is superficial or fleeting.

Mostly, I will listen for the jungle drums. They seem to speak most clearly of all, a constant reminder of what could and should be. They sing of things freely given, and lie just beyond the back fence, hidden within the song which I call home.

Coyote Songs

*T*he coyote symphony came in the wee hours, beginning as a solo voice mourning at the moon and soon joined by the entire Montana chorus. It was one of those warmer evenings we have had of late, the temperature barely at the freezing mark, and I might have missed the performance had not the window been open a crack. The soft breath of a chill breeze makes for good sleep beneath Granny's quilt.

Buffett the wolfhound, my happy malcontent who has proven in the last few months that he has about as much interest in coyotes as a beaver has in algebra, pulled himself awake and offered up a half hearted woof. He then sauntered to the couch and plopped down as only a 150 pound wolfhound can. I came out of a half doze and peered through the window. The hairy cousins of the children of the night were singing their little hearts out under a wet velvet sky.

I walked outside in bare feet for a better look, and seeing nothing but shimmering night and the skeleton silhouette of bare-limbed trees, leaned back for a listen. Magnificent, I thought. They sing the oldies but goodies. Coyotes may be scoundrels and thieves, but they do have hellaciously nice voices.

As the feet started to feel a tad numb, I ventured back inside and sat in the chair by the window. Buffett was still oblivious to all, dreaming the dream of the innocent and perpetually hungry, and I was in a state of contentment. Lighting the old kerosene lamp which sits on the shelf, a gift from my parents, I watched the flickering shadows dance in time to the yip and howls of the four legged carolers. A good night for tired dogs and wailing critters and long haired writers who have temporarily misplaced their ticket on the train of thought. A good night to regroup, I thought. A good night to remember.

Memory is a funny thing, and sometimes the simplest events are the kick required to make the gears mesh and the cogs turn. I remembered a time long ago, 14 years old sitting high on the Ford 6000 tractor, when a massive Missouri coyote calmly padded behind the plow, searching the turned earth for bugs or mice or whatever squirming vermin would suffice as mid-day snack. I remembered, on that same afternoon in that same dusty field, a turkey buzzard sitting on a fence post, eyeing the corpse of a bloated cow (I think it must have been lightning stuck) which lay on the banks of a neighbor's ditch. It was the same day I found the hunk of meteorite, a chunk of odd rock flecked with odder metals which still graces a spot by the old wagon wheel in my folk's back yard.

The coyotes sang and I remembered. I thought of old friends and old loves, some living and some dead, some recently found, some lost forever and some lost only to me. I sank back into the days of sledding on an upturned car hood and speeding down a pond dam on my bike. I reveled in the memory of driving too fast and singing too loud and feeling the tan burn deep from the deck of a tiny catamaran on a forgotten New Year's Day. Images flooded back of catfish bearing down into the murky depths, bass breaking the surface for a grasshopper and snook taking a fresh shrimp while a raccoon cracked oysters on a hidden mangrove island. I thought of trout jumping and a windy canyon and the bugs hovering with the thickness of storm clouds.

The lamp was flickering lower and the acappella voices of the outdoors were fading away. I remembered the past and thought about the present. The future I ignored, for I have quit trying to predict such things and really wouldn't want to even if it was possible. Why spoil the surprise?

The mountains, hooded with a monk's cowl of purest white, stood silent sentinel as always, eternal and all knowing. The wind kicked up a bit, and I took one last look before closing the window. Buffett slept on, dreaming of logs to chew and rabbits to chase and the inevitable tugs of war that the next day would bring.

I returned to bed, pulled high the old quilt and contemplated just a few more things before my eyes and mind shut down for the night. I had survived another year, I would see another day. A birthday had passed and I was blessed with a family that cared and good friends and fine times. The simple things, little by little, were becoming the important things.

One last yelp bit through the dark. In his sleep, Buffett answered with another lackadaisical woof. I realized that it wasn't turkey of parades or Pilgrim tales that make one thankful. It was life itself. Coyote songs and sleeping dogs and moonlit nights and mountains that touch the clouds. I think it would risk irritating the fates to wish for anything more.

I sent a silent word of thanks to the wild ones who were by now loping hills far away, singing only for themselves and those with the need to listen.

It is good to remember, I thought. It is better to remember why.

Sally

Her name was…well…I guess her name doesn't matter.

What does matter is that she was one of the handful of people on this planet whom I ever truly loved. Maybe the person I loved the most and the best. She was tall, brazen and philosophical. Possibly the most gentle person I ever met. Possibly the most realistic. For a long time we were best friends. For a short time we were lovers.

She adored monkeys, antiques, Elvis Costello and the beach. She was beautiful, a genius, golden bronze from head to toe in the way that only beach people can be. She was a bit over six foot tall, a hot shot photographer. She never realized (or was subtle enough never to mention) that I slept through 90% of "Dances With Wolves" on our first date. That's class, at least to my way of thinking.

It was years ago, thousands of miles away. Another place, another time. A place where the sub-tropical aromas caressed us with the seductive smells particular to the offshoot Gulf tradewinds. A time that, now, seems a half remembered dream. She introduced me to beauty, wind chimes, the music of Andreas Vollenweider, and how to arrange my cut-rate bamboo furniture so it didn't look stupid. I introduced her to Silverado cabernet, Ozark philosophy and a large black dog with the personality of Maurice Chevalier and the brains of Albert Einstein.

She named my first magazine column, stealing it off a stupid little novelty coffee cup which I had given her, and dropping the idea into my former editor's mind during a photo shoot.

I hated the name. I still use it. The photos she took still hang on the wall. A miniature, red 1930's Royal typewriter draped with an Indiana Jones jacket bought at a Monkey Wards in Joplin, Missouri way before Indy was even a gleam in the eye of George Lucas. I still wear the jacket. The red Royal still works.

She never believed I loved her. Or, maybe she did. It doesn't matter.

I fed her fajitas and shrimp, salsa, garlic and wine on my deck, popping in Joni Mitchell tapes in between a few random strands of Mozart and Dave Brubeck. I fed her poems and stories and songs which no one, save us, will ever read. Sometimes I wonder if she still has them, those first drafts so precious to me and yet so worthless to others. We compared our childhoods, hers on the far continent (that land of Arthur and Guinevere, Benny Hill and Monty Python) and mine on the near, and found them so similar as to be frightening.

The orange blossoms were in bloom. We talked, we laughed, and the first time she mentioned his name I knew we were doomed. The eyes...you can always tell by the eyes. My heart died that night. Died in a way that the pretty rose on your kitchen table is suddenly pretty no more. It died for a long time.

The dog, realizing my intentions and desperation, charmed her as only a large black dog with the personality of Maurice Chevalier and the brains of Albert Einstein can charm. We did our best. We were in love. We hoped to win her heart.

We lost.

She's married now to a very fine fellow who was somewhat more than my acquaintance and somewhat less than my friend. For them, odd as it sounds, I wish nothing but excitement, ecstasy and full tilt happiness.

The reason, and this may sound selfish, juvenile and egocentric, is because I've finally found the same thing. Not so much with a person, but more with a place.

Corny? Yeah, you'll probably think that. Still, it's true. I'm here because I fell in love with this tiny Montana valley.

Fly by night is not my style, although admittedly I've flown many a coop, and yes, some of them by moon's half light. I've been privileged to live in many places (someone always needs a cheap scribbler) but I've never seen anything like this. I'm in love with a snow-swept Montana valley and all that surrounds it. Call me stupid, call me a romantic. I've lost my heart, something I swore I'd never again do. I'm glad.

"You can be in-love," the tall, English photographer girl with the deep tan once told me, "or you can be in-fatuated. Knowing the difference is the key."

For once, maybe the first time since that long ago phone call on a dark Saturday night, I know the difference.

My old compadre, the black dog with the personality of Maurice Chevalier and the brains of Albert Einstein, is sadly gone to Black Lab heaven. Now I have an Irish Wolfhound puppy who seems to take kindly to snorting at geese and deer and the acrid smell of woodsmoke in the air. The days in the sub-tropics (or the Ozarks, or Idaho or a whole slew of other places) are done as well. Robert Frost once said, "we have miles to go before we sleep." I'm far from ready for nap time.

That girl, the tan one, the girl who chose not to know that I loved her so deeply, would understand. She would comprehend that for the first time in many years, my aim is true. I look at the mountains, run with Buffett in the clear morning air, say hello to the sunrise and thank the fates for allowing me to stumble across a land of such beauty.

Yes…my aim is finally true.

I am home.

Well Met

*I*t is a Tuesday night, and for some odd reason, I find myself contemplating the world of romance. Not unusual, perhaps, when living in a place where the magnificent legacy of Cervantes is as common as the antelope's mad dash or the beaver's slap of a tail. Of such things are love made, of such things are a fine life constructed, and the poets sometimes forget that there is more enchantment in an elk's snort than all the Harlequin novels ever printed. Iambic pentameter and lofty prose cannot match the squeal of a 1,000 feeding bats, and as for the silent swish of the white tail as it effortlessly clears five wires…forget it. Words are powerful, they can paint brilliance, but their strength can never match reality.

Romance is not a topic with which I often break bread. Too many miles on this scarred up body, too much time spent in solo thought. Experience broadens not only one's horizons, but as well the suspicion glands, and I have spent an abundance of years and effort giving that almost emotion a wide berth. Not ambivalent, at least not totally, but the hermit aspect of my make-up includes high walls and pointy shards of wire which serve to keep romance at arm's length..

Stupid, I know, but gut reflexes have no brain. You see, the kid avoids emotional stuff as a rule, for his radar has been proven faulty too often in the past. No doubt I received a cut-rate system which had been booted out of NORAD, a green screen whose flashing blips signify nothing but pathways and potentials. It's a dream radar, and in matters of the heart such technology is not to be trusted.

Can the leopard change his spots? It is a question a friend and I pondered endlessly in the old days. She thought yes, I thought no. A leper can change his spots, I would say, however the internal functions, the bed rock of personality, is set in stone.

In truth, I no longer believe that. People and a land and wild critters of fur and feather have brought about a transformation of sorts. Age teaches silent lessons, and the only thing set in stone, is stone.

Well met...that is the phrase of the old days, bestowed in greeting upon one who has performed an act of bravery or kindness or simple humanity. It is a good phrase, much more telling than our modern hellos, how are ya's, and whatcha up to? Civilization, for all its benefits, has perhaps caused us to lose our sense of appreciation for little things...the pretty smile, the fluttering eye, the enthusiasm of a new day's dawn and those who show style and grace for their own sake.

As I say, it is a Tuesday night, and for some odd reason, my mind has turned to romance. You see, it comes in many shapes and sizes. I hear it in the gentle breeze outside my window, the one which allows me to eavesdrop upon the speech of rustling leaves. I see it in the tiny Wolfhound, now at a sturdy 100 pounds, as he shreds a bundle of knotted socks and rawhide bones. I feel it in the sun, watching it drop towards the western mountains, sinking slowly in a seductive dance of light and clouds and...there is no other word...magic!

It could be any number of things, but there it is, nonetheless. For that I'm grateful. In this place that we live, this land of untamed thoughts and stream borne dreams, how could it be otherwise?

Well met...this valley...it's people.

Well met.

Playing Chess With A Cat

*I*t was a dark and smoky night, a little before All Hallows Eve if memory serves. The band was too loud, the crowd too thick. I had ventured out against my better instincts, but the need for perspective overcame the desire for solitude. Although I much prefer silence over the discordant buzz of grasping chit-chat, there are times when even the most anti-social of hermits requires human interaction.

I spied an unoccupied table in a far corner, bee-lined my way across the floor. Shields up, sensors locked, I began to eavesdrop on the seekers of fun and frolic. Five minutes later, boredom set in. No place is more lonely than a crowded room, and the thrill of social voyeurism is transitory at best.

I was preparing to leave when the cat appeared.

"Weren't you going to say hello," she asked, instantly perceiving that I was immersed in a one man version of hide and seek. I half muttered an answer, realizing as I spoke that my social batteries were long overdue for a charge.

"You looked busy," I replied in brilliant riposte, trying to avoid those hypnotic eyes. A word of advice. Never get in a stare down with a cat. You'll lose.

I had not expected familiar faces that night, particularly not one as familiar as hers. She smiled, making a joke while attempting to attach some fake Halloween cob-webs to my jacket. An appropriate move, I thought. The perfect fashion accessory for one who is attempting to fade into the woodwork. We spoke trivialities for a few minutes, and she glided away. A part of me wanted her to come back.

I thought of her as the cat, for that is how she perceived herself. It was fitting. The flashing eyes, stubborn will and desire to do exactly as she pleased were the very personification of feline. Frustrating at times, maddening and yet strangely alluring. Her movements were gliding and quiet, yet a razor edged wit consistently waited to pounce. Her waters ran both still and deep, however on occasion they transformed into a boulder strewn stretch of rapids.

I'd known the cat for about a month, having shared conversation, laughter, chicken cordon bleu and a sense of mutual confusion. I think we were in joint bafflement, using our verbal fencing matches as insulation against personal revelation. We really knew very little about each other, and what we did know was doled out in tentative bits and pieces. We were both uneasy with such things, a bit leery of human nature's darker side.

Suddenly, the cat was back at my table.

"Sorry I don't have more time," she said.

"It's ok," I answered. "That's really not why I'm here."

When dealing with a cat, one must tread softly. Their ways are foreign to mortal man. Cats decide in their own time, choosing their few companions only after much consideration. They are mysterious, seductive and aloof, yet also loyal and compassionate. One does not possess a cat, to even try is a lesson in futility.

The eyes flashed. Maybe she was laughing, maybe not.

I soon left that dark and smoky place, slipping away without a good-by. It wasn't a snub, just the knowledge that, despite the fact that we circled each other with a questioning eye and wary stance, the cat and I would meet at a later time. For the moment, I was content to wait.

Besides, it's not like there was a choice. When playing chess with a cat, the cat always has the first move.

There was ample time, I thought.

I never saw her again.

The Mirror

*O*n the hill I saw a mirror. Perfect, flawless, polished to a blinding sheen by the rays of the rising sun, it reflected that which it was given.

So it is with beauty.

So it is with time.

As I gloried at the sight of the mirror, I saw a young old man attempting to climb the hill. Seemingly obsessed with reaching this prize, veins pounding in his temples, drenched with the efforts of his toil, I wondered at his folly. Did he seek this timeless mirror for his own? Did he yearn to possess that which was not to be possessed, and yet is possessed by all? What arrogance. What ignorance. How could he fail to understand the nature of the mirror? He had but to look, for the mirror reflected that which it was given.

So it is with pride.

So it is with fear.

But never once did the young old man raise his head. He refused to take the soft green path which so willingly was offered. Instead, he tackled the hill with reckless abandon. He scrambled and fell as his palms bloodied against boulders. He stumbled and tripped in pools left by the night's gentle rain. He berated the Gods for their torture, envisioned himself as the creator of his own soul. Placed himself on a pedestal above universal plans.

He did not realize that he could simply walk to the side. He did not realize that he was also part of the plan.

And all the while the mirror reflected that which it was given.

So it is with arrogance.

So it is with faith.

Finally, battered and worn, he reached the summit of the hill and lay at the base of the great mirror. He tried to wrench it from its site. It would not move. He smashed scarlet hand prints against its face. It would not shatter. He raised his fists to the past, cursed the present, laughed in the face of the future. In his desperation he sought to change the course of the sands of time, soar against the winds of change. The sands merely shifted at his feet. The winds blew him to the edge of the precipice.

Finally, he gazed into the mirror. Face an ashen white, the young old man wept. Maybe he understood.

Flawless, perfect, reflecting only those things placed before its vision, the mirror returns all which it is given.

Look into the mirror, feel the past, see the present, open yourself to the future. Sight or blindness are our highways, free will and faith our only guidance. We can see all, or merely the tiny pieces of our choosing.

Gaze deep, for the inner reflection is the most telling mirror of all. Recorded upon its face is the epic chronicle of our time on this planet. Pleasures, pains, loves, deaths. All we have known, all we have done, all we are yet to do. No vestige of existence is blocked. Our eyes may close, we may turn our backs in ignorance…but still we know.

The mirror of the soul hides no secrets. It returns that which it is given. We, each the guardian of this treasure, consistently flawed, often imperfect, have but to look inside for truth. When in darkness, such mirrors tell all. They can reflect nought but that which they have been given.

So it is with love.

So it is with life.

Dawn's Early Light

*I*t is the deep cold, snow pounding the mountains while the land of The Bear Trap lies sleepy beneath but a mere inch or two of white. The mercury screams out 20° below at 4:10 a.m. this morning, a fact I know too well as that is the usual hour when wolfhound Buffett prefers an outdoor nature call. Barefoot and shirtless, 90% asleep, I open the door and send him on his way. Ten minutes later, not hearing his usual knock, I peer out the frost-laden pane.

Shoes, shirt and a trip into Siberia are required. It is embarrassing for one's beloved dog to stand frozen to a tree. The neighbors might talk.

It is the deep cold, the type that rushes through the high meadows and rips the peaks as it creeps into the heart and lays black ice on the mind. It is February, the time when leap years vault from the calendar and old bones creak with the bitter chill of tired remembrance. It is February, hyperborean detour on the Bifrost Bridge. It is February, the dark month, a time of year I should love for its solitude but that for some unknown reason gives me the Asgard blues.

Oddly enough, out in the parts of the world folks call real, this bleak period of cabin fever and unfulfilled hopes is dedicated to lamps of love which would be better lit in Spring. Maybe that is appropriate, maybe not. Sometimes things just get weird.

Buffett The Wolfhound and I are celebrating Valentine's Day together this year, much in the same manner that Crow the Lab and I did in years past. This is a good thing. Self and canines, both those present and past, long ago learned that such seasons are not of our realm. Unfortunately, we never learn the lesson quite well enough. We know that our universe is not one of the tandem hitch, are well aware our respective self-images revolve around a life of rampant independence free of constraint or imaginary bonds. Still, with regret, we slip and slide on the treacherous path and are forced to re-educate ourselves on an annual basis.

Not a selfish thing, quite the contrary. When it comes to the world of romance the dogs and I immerse ourselves fully in the contradictory state of idealistic cynicism. We contemplate such stuff, but try our best to avoid action. Being merely human (or merely canine) our philosophy generally falters. One should avoid strong drink, for it make you shoot at tax collectors and miss. On the same token, one should never make irrevocable decisions when tired or hungry.

We become bull pragmatists in February, disappearing from sight even more often than is our usual reclusive nature. We are doubtful of the concepts promoted by 18th century English poets. We would no sooner engage in Valentine's Day festivities than an atheist would attend Christmas Mass. St. Valentine's legacy is right and fine for those who have chosen the more stable path, but as a mountain man once told me, the cliff's edge is designed for single file.

I suppose this rant has surfaced because of an odd footrace in which I compete against myself. Having crossed the finish line here at the third vertebra of the backbone of the world, beginning a new journey, I wrongly assumed that the footsteps of yesterday had sought other contests as well. I was wrong. My past recently caught up. Several past loves have mysteriously appeared on my doorstep in recent weeks, all with honest and probing questions.

"How is your social life?" said the girl behind door number one.

"I made a mistake," said the girl behind door number two.

"I no longer want to shoot you," said the girl behind door number three.

Some of these doors I do not mind opening. The ones in which the red hot flames of love and anger have burned to cinders, those that offer friendship and the bonds built of shared history, are welcomed with open arms. Other doors bring mostly confusion. Some questions I can answer, others are more tricky. Hopefully I have become less self-deluding than in years past, for I can now say with a degree of certainty that my life, my road, is based upon ideas and imagination and the dream done solo. Possibilities always exist, that cannot be denied, however the leopard cannot change his spots without radical surgery.

But such is the stuff of February, the puzzling month of lovers. I do not see it, and tend to feel that this darkest time of winter would better operate under the premise of "to thine own self be true." Doors of future open and doors of past close. You never really walk all the way through those portals, you know, and far off in the distance you can often still hear the creaking hinges. At times you yearn for them. Regretting past actions you strain to return to the before and listen more clearly. At other times you run with winged feet. That's the way life is. We are all shaped, molded and formed (or bent, spindled and mutilated) by our experience.

It is a fine thing to look at the past in a new light. It is a poor thing to examine it by the flickering candle of times long gone. Reading in the dark leads to impaired vision. Reading between lines in the dark makes you blind.

Wolfhound Buffett scratches at the door once again. It is 6:17 A.M. and my peanut bladdered dog once more feels the call. Barefoot and shirtless I open the door. The wind stings. It is cold outside.

Dress warmly in February. Avoid hypothermia of the soul.

The icy winds of yesterday should not be confronted with a naked heart.

Ill Winds

*T*he wind blows hard in Montana's Madison Valley this morning, hurricane force gusts which crack the cottonwood limbs with the sounds of gunfire and threaten to lift the roof from its moorings. Frigid gales slide between the numerous cracks and tears in my tar-paper castle, surprisingly less on the ancient log side of the house than the more modern frame side. I crank the oil burner another notch and stick my frigid toes under the wolfhound. We huddle together and watch the gray sky slide down the eastern slope of the Tobacco Root Mountains like lava towards Pompei.

I hate ill winds. They curl the hair and darken the mind and send the hermit of the Madison scurrying for the solace of deep quilts and long books. In most weather—blizzards, rain squalls or sunny skies—I can find a sense of joy. I adore watching lightning caress the peaks just a few short miles from my hovel. I like it even better when I'm sitting on one of those peaks, raging campfire sending smoke signals to the sky as mountain goats play tag on a sheer rock face. Most winds are refreshing, even those that have at various times caught me mid-lake in a leaky canoe or trying to stake down a tent before the canvas rips from my hands and seeks freedom over cliff's edge. I like their feel, their strength, the invisible power that drops from nowhere simply to make us recall our place in the grand scheme of it all.

Ill winds such as this are another story. They blow things away, blow them so far and distant that they may never return. Today they blow a person out of my life, send her winding not only down a distant high-way and out of my valley, but more sadly, down a new path and out of my life.

I remember once hearing a story of ancient mariners, something to the effect that it was bad luck to whistle while sailing the high seas. Supposedly, the story goes, the ill winds were attracted by the sounds of happiness, roaring down from the heavens in an attempt to punish those who took for granted the power of nature, those whose cares were too few. Black skies and blasts of power were the price for expressing too much joy and too little respect in the face of the gods.

I have a tendency to think that, like most old stories, this tale is human analogy. Don't become careless when times are fine, for even in fine times there is work to be done. Don't collapse yourself into good fortune, for a certain degree of vigilance, a wary appreciation of the unknown, is a necessity in life. Protect what you have, for the rust of apathy will find it's way into the smallest corners.

I will not bore you with the story. Suffice it to say we were both Southerners, which if you've ever met one, should speak volumes. Southerners don't have problems, they have patterns. They also have layers of armor and believe a hefty plate of deep fried catfish is a more appropriate curative for confusion than any amount of endless discussion. Then again, confusion isn't strictly a southern thing; it's simply a malady shared by many of us who have led wandering and fractious lives. We're reluctant perfectionists who aren't exactly sure what we seek, and are afraid that if we found it, we might not know it or even want it. We're not ambivalent, just tired of making the wrong choices and screwing up.

Whatever the case, when the tempers flared, we slung our verbal daggers without warning or mercy. Yesterday, sad at what seemed lost, we raised the white flag. Neither wanted to point the sword in our parting. Maybe it will be better in the spring, we agreed, not really believing but not really sure. Hermits are poor at opening their doors. Once they do, they are loathe to close them. Making the leap of faith is difficult in the first place. Being forced to leap back, to return the state of things before, is difficult.. However, the leap must be taken nonetheless. The ill wind demands it.

But for just a little while longer, though the ills winds blow and the cold times beckon, my mind contemplates far-away spring. That is a season I love, a season that will arrive sure as the sunrise, a season of dreams. It is a wondrous time that seems to last forever.

Other equally wondrous times last but for a blink of the eye. In such cases I suppose the trick is to appreciate the beauty of their moment and cherish the fond memories that will, inevitably, fade into the sepia tones of yesterday. No season is forever, nor should it be. Enjoy the good times, find meaning in the bad. Be thankful for the small miracles, for they are the best of all.

Seasons come and seasons go. Still, the voices in the ill wind tell me that some seasons come but once.

Those are the ones I will remember best.

Last Halloween At The Spader Farm

Grant and Dolly Spader were the embodiment of Jack Spratt and his anonymous wife. He was tall and gaunt, a skin covered skeleton with a thick shock of unruly white hair. She was short and fat, always wearing a crazy, gap toothed smile. At the time I figured that both were well into their third century of life, but in retrospect I'm certain that neither was a day over 150. I was eight, which may explain the error.

Like many people who've spent a couple hundred years way back in the sticks, the Spaders had pretty much lost sight of reality. They weren't dangerously insane, but just whacked enough that these days they would be tossed either in the loony bin or a real secure old folks home. The Spaders were kind and generous, but to use the local vernacular, a few bricks shy of a load.

We always had to stop at the Spader farm on Halloween. It was my Mom's idea, and one with which I never agreed. In the sticks, at least back in the days when Halloween meant something more than a busy night at the hospital x-ray lab, courtesy required stopping at every house in the township. To ignore a home was an insult, a social faux pas which would be repeated all over the party lines by morning.

Still, I hated the mandatory Grant and Dolly visit. I hated it for reasons far greater than the fact that they were just as likely to dump finishing nails or an outdated driver's license in your bag instead of candy corn and Snickers. They were scary in the way that real life is scary, a View-Master still life into one of many potential futures. That's heavy stuff for anybody, let alone a pre-adolescent redneck.

But never was a Halloween as bad as the year Grant got gangrene. Somehow he'd managed to ram a rusty pitchfork in his leg, and in the manner of ancient country recluses, had chosen to simply ignore the wound. Finally, some neighbors hauled Grant to the Doc. It was too late. Age and a rotting foot would soon take him. The Doc wrapped Grant up and sent him home with pain pills. It would be his last Halloween, so of course we had to pay our respects.

Dressed as a 90 year old woman (The truth comes out. I was an eight year old cross-dresser) my Mom drove self and older sibling to the Spader place. She looked at us gravely and gave one piece of advice.

"If he asks if you'd like to see his foot, say no." Mom always has had an odd sense of humor.

We trudged to the Spader house. We knocked on the Spader door. The gap toothed crazy Spader smile appeared. Grant and Dolly made scary noises, he made mention of a flesh eating hoot owl which lived in the cedar tree by their front door. He asked if we'd like to look at his foot. We declined, although I think my brother really wanted to. They stuck wormy apples in our bags and were preparing to drop in a pair of bi-focals when we proffered our thanks and beat brush back to the car. Mom casually drove us to the next place with nary a question.

That was the last time I went out on Halloween. That's strange, but then again, I was a strange kid. Some things never change. After that night, the talk of ghosts and goblins and vampires and flesh eating hoot owls seemed as distant as the moon. It was my first glimpse of the frailty of innocence, and that's a much more frightening sight than anything available from H.P. Lovecraft or Stephen King.

But no more frightening than the here and now.

Halloween used to be known as a night when parents indulged their children with the potential reality of childhood fears. Unfortunately, such a practice has become too dangerous. Trick or treat is virtually extinct. The nuts and weirdoes and criminal psychotics have screwed it up. That's a shame, for as with most things, lessons come when you least expect them.

I feel sorry for kids these days, for they have to face dangers that I never imagined. I used to get mad that a dying old man had caused me to grow up a little quicker than I'd like. That I'd missed a few years of innocent fun due to a first hand glimpse at the downside of life. I'm not mad anymore. Grateful maybe, but never mad. My only regret is that kids of the now have to live in a sanitized and regulated world where real fears take away the possibility of infinite imaginings. Innocence may pass quickly and without warning, but one should at least have the chance to lose it naturally and in their own time.

To the Spaders…Happy Halloween. You are missed.

Into The Dark

*T*he carnie man was somewhere between 45 and 70 years of age, an amalgamation of tattoos, scars, bad teeth and multiple personalities. He scampered out of camera range, looked around and noticed an audience of one. For some reason, crazy people are drawn to me like mosquitoes to a bug zapper. It must be pheromones, some sort of body chemistry thing.

Just for a second he was quiet, his eyes boring a hole in the side of my skull. I couldn't see those eyes, covered by black shades as they were, and didn't really want to. I could sense the twitching spasms, the wild lack of focus. Something was percolating behind those hidden orbs, and it sure as hell wasn't the comforting aroma of mountain grown Folgers. This brain had more occupants than a Manhattan subway at rush hour.

"Can't let 'em take my picture. I'm still wanted in two countries," he blurted, a fine trail of something unidentifiable running from the left corner of his mouth. He began to stare once again, the maniacal look holding steady until one of those countless upstairs residents butted in with a sudden conversational tangent. "Everybody brings me their knives to sharpen."

"Why's that?" I asked, curious as to which personality would offer up a soliloquy on the finer points of honing an edge, something of an irony since this old boy had apparently gone over the edge years before. I hoped the respondent would be somebody cool. Considering the situation, Rod Serling might be nice.

"I don't just put on an edge. They're razor sharp," he beamed, hesitating once again as the mental doorbell hit a clunker. "The U.S. government keeps telling them I'm deceased, but Red China wants me. That girl up there has a little pocketknife."

Ok, it wasn't Serling. Still, I was definitely getting my money's worth on this trip to the Twilight Zone.

What function the carnie man fulfilled at the midway of the Eastern Idaho State Fair was a mystery, although pestering me seemed a job he took quite seriously. Frankly, my curiosity was fading. I've never been comfortable in front of groups.

I moved a few steps away. The one man gallery followed.

"Fifty six of us started and only two's left alive," he proclaimed, making me wonder if the mysterious duo of which he spoke was napping up in cerebellum mansion while I made small talk with the hired help. He displayed a hairy arm covered with what appeared to be either a serious skin disorder or a faded, homemade tattoo of indiscernible nature. He waved a dirty hand in my face, pointing and gesturing as if the blue blob of ink on the skin canvas was some sort of transubstantiated Rosetta Stone, a cryptographer's key to unlocking the secrets of his wandering message.

"You better damn well believe it," he muttered with raised eyebrows, now expounding on some other topic. He leaned close, a tsunami of Wild Turkey fumes assaulting my nostrils. He winked slyly and grinned, showing off his half a dozen rotting teeth. "It's the God's own truth!"

Truth and fiction, I think, are highly subjective. Some try to tell it, others avoid it like the plague, many don't know the difference. On the carnival midway of a fair, the entire concept takes on a different dimension from the rest of society. The authentic and the spurious get all mixed up, which is, perhaps, the largest part of the midway's dark attraction. It's leather clad carnie girls, the sadistic grins of the lost souls who run the Tilt-A-Whirl, those evil outcasts who smile sweetly and speed up the twisting saucers as little kids lose their lunch and old men grasp at their chests. It's latter day James Deans, posing rebels without a cause but with Stetsons, clutching their young girlfriends in a Vulcan death grip of possessiveness. It's the grease paint leers and red nose smirks of the devil clowns.

It's a Stephen King scratch and sniff. On the midway, all types come together in a parody of our mundane and "normal" culture. A nice place to visit, but....

The carnie man staggered down the gravel path between the carnie tents, which would later be filled with sound of carnie barkers and cheap Taiwanese carnie toys. He muttered a few half heard curses at a bag of stuffed Barney the Dinosaurs, ground to a shaky halt, and remembered his manners.

"Well, gotta go," he said, head bobbing up and down like one of those spring loaded dogs in the back window of a Plymouth. I wondered if his eyes would blink when he turned the corner. They didn't, and he disappeared behind the tent and out of my life.

You know, somewhere in the mass of misfiring synapses and neural short circuits there was a story. This had once been a human being, after all, and I'm sure he had a tale to tell. Unfortunately, too much travel into dark alleys has a tendency to make one a bit cynical. I'd heard tales such as his before, too often if the truth be known, and had neither the time nor inclination for another. Some truths are better left as fiction. Some realities are merely boring.

A 16 year old girl (she could have been 20 or 30 or 40) had been listening intently to the dialogue between self and the carnie man, the same girl who presumably had the little pocket knife. She gave me a wink and an inviting look, twisting seductively on the ladder where she was arranging cheap Rod Stewart posters, vividly displaying dirty blonde hair and tight cut-offs and a well filled tank top which a third grader couldn't have squeezed into. She motioned me closer, the skull tattoo on her left forearm grinning wildly in anticipation.

I grinned back and strolled slowly towards the exit, whistling a Bob Dylan tune, deciding that it takes all types to make a world and all experiences to make a life.

Beyond the fairgrounds the sun was shining. I stopped at a kid's lemonade stand for a five cent drink, giving the seven year old a buck and watching his eyes light up.

For this day, I'd seen enough of the dark.

Beam Me Up

*H*is name was John "Laser" Beam. He was tall and gangly, skin the color of chalk, with an outrageous unkempt mess of bright orange hair that would have put a bunch of carrots to shame. Laser was deaf in one ear, and as a result his speaking voice was delivered in a key virtually indecipherable to that of Mickey Mouse. The kids called him Laser, but if I recall they also labeled him Frog and Toad and about 1,000 other monikers unsuitable for print in a family publication or even this one. Laser got beat up a lot.

Laser's family was weird, a bunch of Holy Rollers of the vein that were too unathletic to jump pews but didn't mind gnashing their teeth, speaking in tongues or handling the occasional pit viper. One sister, a fat, frumpy dishwater blond with the IQ of a turnip, spent most of her hours trying to pick up any 13 year old boy who wasn't totally disgusted by her odd manner, off-set eyeballs and generally inbred appearance. She was 19 at the time. Connie later married, if memory serves, the dim-wit pervert son of the half-wit owner of the local beer joint/pool hall/grease pit. I believe they had kids, which just goes to prove that the Chinese are much wiser on the subject of population control than us. I think Connie got beat up a lot.

Another sister was somewhat more attractive, a little more bright, and had the tendency to chase relentlessly after any high school drop-out that had a homemade tattoo and could prove he'd done time. Chenelle was the bane of my family's existence, at least as far as telecommunications were concerned. Rural Missouri was still in the dark ages known as the party line days, and Chenelle and her love du jour would tie up Mr. Bell's invention for hours on end, just breathing heavy and muttering classic comments like "What's wrong?" At least that's what Chenelle would say on the various times I listened. I'm sure her Neanderthal boyfriends had yet to evolve to that point where the power of speech was even a far-off dream. I hear Chenelle later married and got beat up a lot.

I used to take care of the Beam dogs whenever the family was skittering off to a tent revival or reptile farm or something. They were hyper little mutts, but in my mind most all dogs are good ones. Maybe they got beat up a lot but I don't think so. Although the Beam family tree didn't fork, although their gene pool was about two inches deep, they never struck me as dog beaters. I think Laser's high pitched voice probably just afflicted the pups at some ultra-sonic level comparable to a dog whistle and they had gone mildly insane.

I didn't have anything particular against the Beams, but I was never too fond of them either. Frankly, they flat out gave me the willies. For one thing they weren't very good neighbors, being transplanted city folks who, like many city folks, were not versed in the arts of courtesy and civilization. Plus, as I said, the Beam daughters weren't exactly cute. None of the city folks that moved to our area ever had cute daughters, now that I think about it, but that's another story. Maybe all the urban adults with cute daughters had seen Chain Saw Massacre or Deliverance and figured it wise to stick to home turf. Laser was the only Beam I could really tolerate, and only then if I wore earplugs. He was something of a mutant and a colossal screw-up, granted, but that wasn't really his fault. Sometimes the gene pool plays Russian Roulette and there's not a damn thing anyone can do, except the Chinese, and again, that's another story.

The Beams have been hanging around my mind because of a conversation I was having with a local hermit type the other day. The hermit and I were lamenting the fact that the West is filling up with folks who eat with 27 forks and turn up their nose at anything without a designer label and/or humongous price tag that will impress the buzzards back home.

To make a long story short, we both decided that, of all the languages on planet Earth, we are most incapable of speaking Yuppie.

I suppose I could eventually decipher Yuppie if I sat down with a Kray super-computer and the fabled Yuppie Rosetta stone (discovered on the back of a menu from a New Age coffee house menu that burned down in 1983 just outside of Seattle) but the language has too much posturing, too many lisps, twists, guttural slurs, tongue clicks and a 1,000 other fake nuances that are repulsive to my skin and offensive to my ears. Yuppies talk of BMW's and pasta makers and describe brands of clothing unknown to this poor hermit soul. When I shop for shoes (which is hardly ever) I ask the clerk "got any shoes?" When I shop for shirts (which is less than hardly ever) I say "got any shirts?" I wouldn't know the preferred Yuppie clothing line if it sat up and bit me.

I don't give a damn for chic coffee houses or cutesy restaurants, despise snooty attitudes and condescending debutantes. Critically acclaimed movies bore me, and I'll state for the record that the best thing about that mega-Yuppie film, "The Piano," was that the lead actress was mute in most of it. Give me an Ernest flick any day. I will freely admit that I thrive on red meat, cuss at liberals and do my utmost to humiliate any Yuppie supplicant of the Political Correctness gods.

I had about 10 people come up to me in the last month, all dressed to the nines for their "Nature Experience," all driving a $250,000 hotel on wheels, all asking about a good place to camp. I hope the powers that be will forgive me for giving them directions to the parking lot of the Holiday Inn in Bozeman. The thought of a Winnebago dumping its chemical toilet in my favorite camping spot, a booming stereo or solar-powered TV spoiling the quiet and drowning out the coyotes, is both chilling and sinister. I'm surprised these charter members of the

Church of Latter Day John Denvers didn't ask to use my toothbrush or buy my dog.

The Beams were weird. When I was a kid they gave me the creeps, but at least, unlike Yuppies, they had individual personality. They were people (using the phrase lightly) who slunk into your life and percolated around and made for the thousands of good tales that lead to an interesting life. The Beams, unlike Yuppies, weren't self-aggrandizing, egomaniacal clones. They were bizarre and sometimes grotesque and drove us nuts on a regular basis, but they also had character and class, even if it was odd character and low class. I'll take such traits over false posturing and incessant boasting, the Yuppie way, any day of the week.

I kind of miss the Beams, just like I kind of miss my childhood. These days, they both seem better and purer and more funny than I'm sure they ever were at the time. I suppose that's just the way the clock ticks.

I miss them, no doubt, but I'm glad they both reside elsewhere.

If I could just figure a way to get Yuppies to do the same all would be well.

Hybrid Vigor

*H*arlen Hooper had a technicolor forehead, a 66 Impala with Bondo stalagtites, and an amazing propensity to get on the nerves of all who met him. He always wore a DeKalb Hybrid feed cap, even when he slept or took a shower, and claimed at least six times a day that the cap had once saved his life. I never believed this story, but since Harlen believed it, and both he and it were/are really stupid, I suppose it's worth telling

Harlen's tale began in a small, northern Missouri town which, not coincidentally, was named Hoopertown. Harlen's Great Great Granddaddy had founded the place, and the name he bestowed upon the community speaks volumes about the legendary creative powers of the Hooper clan. Their imagination well had apparently run dry back in the prehistoric days. In scientific terms, the Hooper creative juices had done went and evaporated.

As the story goes, Great Great Gramps lucked into buying 40 acres of land that contained an undiscovered zinc mine, and thus made enough money to get a town named after him. Actually, it's suspected that the name wasn't official until Grandpa Hooper made a sizable donation for the upkeep of a local "Men's Social Club" (which the girls in charge wouldn't let him enter) but this is not a proven fact so I won't mention it. He died in a tragic grain elevator explosion which he caused with his stinkin' cigar, and was the last Hooper to amount to anything, even though he eventually amounted to not much more than a smoldering little pile of wheat ash.

Great Grandpa Hooper must not have been wearing a feed hat on the day the wheat went pow, but I'm not sure even a feed hat would stop the concussive force inherent in a grain dust conflagration. Harlen would no doubt disagree, but as I strongly implied earlier, he was stupid.

Nothing much happened in Hoopertown after Gramps blew the place up. The surviving residents and their descendants just sat around and got old and plunked away at barn swallows with their 22's and chewed their tongues and stuff. The place did make the news a few years back—during the 1993 floods—when all the old graveyards washed out and the burial vaults went floating down the Missouri river. This natural disaster got Hoopertown laughed at extensively, for it's a pretty sorry state of affairs when even the dead folks up and move. Dead person diasporas seem to indicate a dissatisfaction with an area's lack of services and quality of life in general. Real estate values plummeted.

The flood was the most exciting thing that had happened in Hoopertown since the great grain elevator explosion, unless you count the time Harlen's DeKalb Hybrid feed cap saved his life. He claimed his doctor would verify this fact, but I never met the guy and strongly doubt the veracity of any tale spun by a doctor who lives in a VW Microbus. I further suspect that if DeKalb Hybrid feed caps made one invulnerable to intense and traumatic head impact, then the government would make us wear them instead of motorcycle helmets.

Whatever. The story goes like this. Harlen smacked a fence post and went through the window of his Impala—DeKalb Hybrid feed cap first. The DeKalb Hybrid feed cap (allegedly) took the brunt of the force and protected his skull from getting smashed, but did not stop about three Anderson window's worth of glass from making a home in his forehead. This led to the famed technicolor forehead effect I mentioned earlier. The doc in the Microbus (or maybe some drinking buddies of Harlen's, this has always been unclear) took the glass out with a pair of needle nose pliers, but Harlan was left with some nasty scars. Whenever he got agitated his forehead would turn a bright red and pulsate with color. A friend of mine used to make Star Wars light saber noises to go along with this noggin version of the Aurora Borealis. Harlen was never amused.

Of course, we probably wouldn't have ever done nasty things like that to Harlen if he hadn't been such a constant pain and if hadn't insisted on telling us, at least six times a day, about the time a DeKalb Hybrid feed cap saved his life. I haven't seen him for many years, and I doubt if he thinks I'm a very good host. The last time was when he showed up unannounced at my house and wanted to stay for a couple weeks. I made him sleep close to my labrador, Crow, who was getting old and had a bit of a gas problem. It was also a bad summer for fleas, and if you put a piece of typing paper on the floor you could hear the things landing. Harlen lasted most of one night.

I guess I'm writing all this 'cause I recently got news of Harlen. He and his sister Rennie, who used to be cute but now chain smokes Luckies and usually smells like gin, inherited five acres smack in the middle of a defaulted gravel quarry. They were digging around in there for fishing worms one day, and while they didn't hit a bubblin' crude like Jed Clampett, they did uncover an Artesian Hot Springs. Some developers bought them out and I hear they're on easy street.

It's good to hear that old friends have found fortune after years of tragedy. It's also pleasing to know that the Harlen and Rennie have invested their money wisely, rather than blowing it on tanning salon distributorships or Gizzard On A Stick franchises.

I understand they're building a grain elevator.

The Great Ozark Beanfield Massacre

I'd like to say that Delmer Loam's brother was dumb as a rock, however such would be an offense to self respecting rocks the world over. Delmer wasn't exactly what you'd call bright either. He was a greasy haired tough guy who, last time I heard, found out that he wasn't so tough after all. Sticking up a gas station and getting sent to the pen was probably a lesson in humility for Delmer, and I figure he learned lots of valuable prison skills like how to carve soap and make license plates and get tattooed and stuff.

Still, compared to his older brother, Delmer was the next best thing to Albert Einstein or Stephen Hawking or maybe even food dehydrator king Ron Popeel, with the exception that none of those guys ever did time. I do wonder how Popeel avoided it. Anybody who would sell hair in a can or glue two feet of plastic tubing on a cheap Zebco spincasting reel and have the audacity to call it "The Popeel Pocket Fisherman" might deserve some rehabilitative therapy. I guess being a genius inventor demands leniency when you screw the public. And, to give Ron credit, he did redeem himself with the food dehydrator and the Vege-Matic and that doohickey that unscrews tight jar caps.

But Delmer wasn't an inventor, unless inventing a nasty case of B.O. counts, so he went straight to jail and didn't even collect $200. I don't know if he ever got out, and don't really care. We were in high school together, or we were until Delmer dropped out Sophomore year, and I haven't heard beans about him since.

Speaking of beans…

Delmer's dimwit older brother, Farrel, created something of a five minute sensation by devising a crime so stupid that he should get a place of honor in the Museum of Incredibly Stupid Crimes located in Gatlinburg, Tennessee. IE: He ripped off 50 pounds of soy beans from a truck that happened to be sitting at the local diner, took them down to the elevator in a bag, and demanded cash money for his harvest. Of course, Farrel got laughed at severely, detained heavily and the farmer who owned the soybeans decided to prosecute humorously. The farmer who claimed the purloined beans as his own might have been lying. Those beans didn't have scars or distinguishing markings that I could see, and according to the American Bar Association, soybean testimony is rarely accepted in a court of law. Still, they were some farmer's beans, and the general consensus was that if nobody claimed ownership Farrel might have failed to learn his lesson and then gone on to bigger offenses, like swiping corn or watermelons.

At any rate, Farrel went to the slam and thus became the first 50 pound soybean burglar in the history of modern criminology and/or row crops.

There's a moral to this story someplace, but I'm really not sure where it is. It could be something to the effect that crime against soybeans doesn't pay. But, as any farmer will tell you, legalities involving soy-beans, like growing them, don't pay all that well either. The moral could be "a mind is a terrible thing to waste," but since the Loam family didn't have one mind between them that amounted to a hill of beans (beans again) and were pretty much always wasted, that one seems unsuitable as well.

Some gene pools have a low diving board. I guess that's as close to a profound learning experience as will get on this one. I do know that, thanks to Farrel Loam's agriculturally based run-in with the law, I gained a perspective of sorts into the workings of the criminal justice system. His defense was classic.

"It ain't hurtin' nobody," bleated Farrel to Hanging Judge Francis Perrucci, a staunch supporter of the rights of victimized soybeans and other nitrogen emitting plant life. "And b'sides, they wuz insured."

I always wondered what happened to Farrel and his novel grasp of the concept of crop insurance. Hopefully he learned his lesson and didn't marry any first cousins and has a nice, respectable job at the Taco Hut or The White House or someplace suited to his unique talents.

I have a feeling he did well in the futures market.

The Big Bang Theory

*F*red's Diner reached critical mass on Friday the 13th, 1959. The explosion was blamed on gas, which was something of an ironic diagnosis considering the quality of Fred's entrees. The best thing on Fred's menu was salt. The tossed salads were so poor they could only afford 500 Island dressing. Even the catsup stank. The greasy mushroom cloud billowing into that November night sky was auspicious in that it mean old Fred's food was finally hot.

The knowledge of this minor disaster is secondhand, but from a reliable source. My parents were on the scene when Fred's went boom, but a tad preoccupied. My mother was in labor, my father in the last stretch of a 15 mile, high speed race to the county's only hospital. I'm sure he was having more fun than she was. The old man has always been into, shall we say, rather erratic driving. This was fitting since, at the time, he owned an insurance agency. Dad's ability to speed on gravel roads is legendary; I don't even want to talk about the time he bottomed out so hard he knocked the gas tank out of a '67 Impala.

Anyway, as you probably guessed, Mom was in labor with me. I'm recalling this stuff because it's my birthday.

You know, there are many things I look forward to, but birthdays aren't necessarily one of them. They make me moody and surly and prone to public displays of weirdness. This phenomena has nothing to do with age, for despite the prematurely gray hair, I'm not that old. It's not any type of mortality factor, for frankly, I'm amazed I've lived this long. It's not that I live by myself, or that I've yet to become a multi-millionaire. Hermits are happiest by themselves, and most of the people I've known with ostentatious wealth get really bored. It's something else entirely.

I think birthdays make me weirder than normal because they necessitate thoughts of both past and future. As age and experience increase, and one gets a tiny taste of life, you would think that the quest for the novel, the unique, would become increasingly more important. In most cases, it doesn't. A lot of people seem to become complacent with age, quit striving, give up the thoughts of lofty quests and the slaying of dragons. I dislike birthdays not because of hip replacements and excessive graying, but more because I fear becoming the thing I despise. I tremble at the thought of slipping into a glass walled rut of mediocrity. I shudder that I might wake up one day and think things like health insurance or retirement plans are important. The status quo is deadly and boring and deadly boring. It lurks behind every bush.

"I would rather be a superb meteor, every atom of me in magnificent glow, than a sleepy and permanent planet. The proper function of man is to live, not merely exist." Jack London said that, and died two months later. Although over dramatic, the quote keeps running through my head. Is it true? Is it possible? And what am I worried about? A year ago, while working at a good sized publication in Idaho, I predicted that, within a year, I would have a place in Montana, a newspaper, an Irish Wolfhound and some much desired solitude. I got my wish. I love it as much as I thought I would. I just fear that my comfort and happiness will make me stale.

Maybe birthdays are meant to reinforce the belief that life is too short for either regrets or caution. Perhaps they reveal that good things do come to those who wait, but that you should keep track of your time and bill accordingly. Could be they are warning signs, advising you to stay on your toes and keep your eyes open for possibilities and adventure. Most of all, I think they are a reminder to always hold onto your own priorities, rather than accepting the priorities of others.

Losing youth is no big deal. Losing your way is a tragedy.

At any rate, on that Friday the 13th, 1959, Fred's blew sky high at the exact second my parents blew by. Dad, head of the fire department, dropped Mom at the emergency room door and went looking for a firetruck, something he could no doubt drive more recklessly than the family Chevy. When he returned, I was alive and well and no doubt puffing on a Marlboro. I imagine Mom was glad he'd had something to occupy his mind. Although it was an unheard of practice in that place and time, she once mentioned that she thinks this modern day "man in the delivery room" bit is highly obnoxious, more often done to impress the neighbors than out of honest emotion. The folks aren't into political correctness, God love 'em, a trait which they've passed onto me. A good present, that. I treasure it.

The folks still find the events of my birth a bit propitious, until I remind them that the explosion of a tacky diner isn't quite the same as the appearance of a blazing comet or a Christmas star.

They send a cake anyway.

A Resolution In Time

*N*ew Year's Resolutions are rarely worth the bar napkins on which they are spilled. Gonna' quit smoking. Gonna' go to church. Gonna' get down to my original birth weight. Gonna' quit coveting both my neighbor's wife and his chainsaw. Gonna' steer clear of fast cars, loose women, dry wine and wet martinis. Gonna' do this. Gonna' do that.

Gonna' forget all that stuff within a week and fall into the comforting arms of blessed, selective amnesia. Promises one makes to one's self apparently don't count on New Year's Eve, the biggest pseudo-holiday ever invented by those who walk upright. I've never seen the point in all the year end revelry. Hey, even if it was a crummy year I have no desire to go inflict one last jab of the red hot poker on my tortured soul, hanging out with a bunch of amateur guzzlers who, let's face it, pick this one night to renew their fleeting acquaintance with Mr. Jack Daniels.

I hide out on New Year's Eve, which shouldn't come as much of a surprise since I hide out for about 313 of the other days of the year, but when the ball drops I can guarantee that I couldn't be found by a whole kennel of D.E.A. trained, Editor sniffing, psychic dogs with x-ray vision and the power of invisibility.

In my experience, New Year's Eve begins with people all jolly and cheery, but by around 10:30 p.m. the storm clouds are building on the horizon. Rather than celebrate the good things of the preceding months, the well juiced party mammals often contemplate failure and loss and personal slights. They dwell on everything from the failed relationship to the argument over visiting rights with the labrador to that time back in August when the left rear tire blew out during a rain storm. No wonder Father Time is ready to make a hasty exit when the clock strikes 12 bells. The underlying mood is surly enough that Baby New Year would be well advised to acquire a Kevlar bullet-proof vest and a formula bottle full of mace. New Year's Eve is a giant domestic dispute waiting to happen, complete with funny hats.

I know. I know. It's neither politically nor socially correct to bad-mouth a holiday, especially one so well regarded as New Year's. It's not so much the night itself that bothers me as the traits it brings out in folks, traits we all share on some repressed level but to which I'd just as soon remain ignorant. I'm all for making Uncle Budweiser more money, under normal circumstances, but not at the cost of witnessing massive depression, gory car wrecks, the sounds of tootie horns and the flapping of inebriated dirty laundry in the wind.

So you ask, Mr. New Year's Eve Pessimist, just how do you celebrate? Well, to be honest, I don't. It's just not my thing. I never make resolutions, never wear a party hat. Champagne gives me a wicked headache. A boring ol' dude, that's me, sitting around and waiting for the next day when I can slap together a pot of beans and hamhocks, chow down on cornbread and pickle relish, and maybe find a decent football game somewhere.

I suppose, if I was going to make a resolution or ten, they would be highly personal things that have nothing to do with the traditional weight loss, smoking cessation vows. Overwhelmingly non-physical deals involving my modes of behavior and the way I treat both others and myself. That sounds a little serious, but it's really not. Introspection is great, as long as you don't overdo it. Like everyone else there are certain things I don't like about myself, certain behaviors I find offensive or destructive, which I could leave at the side of the road and be the better for. Maybe January 1st is as good a day as any to attempt such premeditated baggage loss. We'll see, but I don't think the day is as important as the sincere desire.

Should such pledges of internal redemption come to pass this week, I won't call them New Year's Resolutions. The very phrase has the smell of failure and triviality, and any change intended to better a life should be regarded with nothing less than major respect.

As I look back, I see that this has been one of the better years in a long while. There have been a few sad and bitter moments, time blips of anger and frustration, but those are just part of life, mistakes which can't be healed or recalled by human means. For the most part it's been a dandy 365. I learned a little, and major regrets can be counted on one hand. I've got friends and family and am doing what I love in a place I want to be. Before I know it, the fish will be biting and I'll be sitting in the canyon under a warm spring sun. Time is something to cherish all year, for it is amazingly fleeting. What it's not is a ten second countdown and the chorus of Auld Lang Syne.

Time is short but the years are long. It's a commodity that trickles away, unknown, like pennies from a torn pocket. You can't stop it, hold it or retard it's inevitable movement. Today we are a child with a pile of blocks, tomorrow we feel the ache in our bones and the twilight chill of tomorrow.

It's a good thing to celebrate the New Year, as long as we celebrate all of it, keeping a sharp focus on the positive and striving to decipher the message of the negative. As long as we appreciate our scant hours just as much in July as on December 31st, as long as we remember the good and assimilate the bad, we'll be just fine.

I don't need a party hat to figure that one out.

Politics As Usual

*M*an must have some inner need for politics, a requirement rating right up there with food, water, oxygen and Andy Griffith re-runs. Although we make arguments to the contrary, say we are sick of all the verbal jabs and mud slinging, it still appears that many of us harbor a secret enjoyment of the conflict. It's similar to the way we buy those tabloid newspapers detailing Elvis sightings, backyard brain transplants and alien baby stories. We watch the show, speak of it endlessly at the dinner table and believe none of it. That's sad.

We have become anesthetized to nearly any comment the wanna' be legislators could hurl at each other. Their raised eyebrows and not so veiled suggestions leave us breathless. Extra-marital affairs, drug use (filmed drug use in the case of the heinous Marion Berry...former twisted mayor of our nation's capitol/den of thieves) and draft dodging are no big deal. The trend towards bad taste and lack of honor continues to escalate, while ol' Tom Jefferson does a reverse gainer with three half twists in his grave.

Professional wrestling has more integrity. Frankly, I'm surprised that some candidate has yet to accuse his opponent of having sex with an underage goat. Stay tuned, friends and neighbors...stay tuned.

Flat out lies are merely something we expect. Matters of personal ethics are not seen as all that important in a candidate, for few of them seem to have any. As I sat and watched the returns last Tuesday night, chomping down on Chinese food and hoping for a good fortune cookie, I was trying to put my finger on just exactly when it was that things got out of control. What day was it when politics changed from a chance to make a difference via elected office to a spitting contest between drooling fabricators of the truth?

I decided it was long before I was born, probably long before anyone currently reading this publication was born. Politics have always been dirty, (Pendergast, Tweed, Grant, Teapot Dome, Watergate...take your choice, there's thousands of 'em) it's just that the technology now exists to beam the dirt directly into our living rooms. Why is this done? Simple. We allow it. The trend will continue until we, as a people, decide we respect honor and courage in our statesmen (as well as in the media that swells like a bloated tick on scandalous ratings and scurrilous head-lines) more than lurid insights into the gutter.

Is it any wonder America is no longer respected abroad? I think not.

I believe most politicians would steal pencils at a sheltered workshop, take candy from babies and lie to our faces. Think about this; HAVE YOU EVER SEEN A POLITICIAN ACTUALLY ANSWER A QUES-TION? I haven't. I've seen them hem and haw and change the subject, but not a damn one of them has the guts to go out on a limb and say what they actually feel. I can't figure how they even decide to get up in the morning, as none seem to be equipped with the decision gene. Politicians, being politicians, will never take a stand until they have determined which way the wind blows. They want to keep their cushy jobs and cushy parking places and cushy secretaries and cushy junkets to places where its warm in the winter. Not wanting to face issues, they attempt to divert us with the exhumation of their opponent's skeletons. That's ok, for the tabloids. That's not ok when its an individual fiddling with our freedoms and tax dollars.

On the other hand, there is a positive side to politics, and the only place it can be found is on a purely local level. I would venture to say that most local politicians volunteer their time for public office out of a sincere desire to serve, to help make a difference. You may not agree with their views, but at least they (for the most part) are trying. There will be mistakes and screw ups and arguments, that's without question. There will also be those who occasionally enter a race to feather their own nest. Still, I like to think that, when it comes down to brass tacks, the small money, non-media campaigns are the only ones which deserve respect. The big time stuff is nothing but another prime time soap opera.

I have little hope for the future of this country, if I base my entire viewpoint on the workings of the federal government. It is incompetent and corrupt and primarily geared towards perpetuation of its own chaotic existence. The desire of federal bureaucrats to expand their control over state and local affairs has been a battle ground since before the Civil War. Make a person (or a village, town, county, city or state) dependent upon the good will of the Great White Fathers in Washington, and they will soon find that their inalienable rights have puffed away like smoke in the breeze.

Always listen to politicians. When they say they are doing something for your own good, prepare to don chain mail, draw sword and wade into the fray. They seek to improve their own well being, not yours.

The name calling, the criminal activities, the muck raking, the sensationalism…It's a wonder any of us vote. I guess that's the only thing that gives me a vestige of hope, the fact that an awful lot of people out there do vote, they do care. They are making a statement of hope, and you can't help but respect that, even if you don't respect the individuals on the tickets. Our inquiring minds extend beyond finger pointing and dirty tricks and the search for Bigfoot. We want educated decisions and clear results from our legislators, not sleaze bag diversionary tactics, shown in 27 inch living color, of what went on behind the bedroom door.

At least, I hope we do.

On Men & Trucks

*E*dward T. Bascomb and I were blasting down the Roy Rogers Turnpike in a 1976 Ford Ranchero with a 454 four barrel, Starsky and Hutch racing stripes and a propensity to suck more oil than a west Texas gusher. We'd left the Ozarks in a bit of a rush, wisely deciding that certain indiscretions are best handled from Oklahoma City. Without going into grisly details, lets just say that some Hillbilly gene pools lack the DNA strand for humor. Distance is the better part of valor.

I power slid into the Kerr-McGee station outside Tulsa for a quart of 50 weight racing oil and a stick of jerky. E.T. gave me an odd look and offered a revisionist suggestion.

"We'd be there by now if we'd brought old '56," he said, referring to his rebuilt Chevy half ton with the Corvette engine, Trans Am rear end and enough body putty to close the ozone hole twice over. "This isn't even a real truck."

E.T. was right. A man should have a truck. It is a deep and burning male need right up their with an unused set of weights, a Bull Worker II, and the complete collection of "Ernest" movies. Unwittingly, my friend had revealed of one of the 14 secrets of the universe.

Men love trucks.

Trucks are less messy than a dog and far less demanding than a girl-friend, or maybe I got that backwards. They never want to go out at 3:00 in the morning, and I've yet to see a Bronco, Blazer or Ram Charger that left panty hose hanging from the shower rod. You never have to de-worm a truck. You never have to be nice to your truck's parents. If your truck decides to dump you, you simply get an estimate and buy another one.

Well, maybe that last one kind of applies to girlfriends too, but you get the idea.

The only thing men like more than trucks are guns, which works out quite nicely since all trucks are born with a gun rack. The South would have won the Civil War if Quantrill's Raiders had owned a couple of S-10's with gun racks. A truck without a gun rack is similar to a bird without wings, which, come to think about it, is usually what happens when a bird meets up with a guy in a truck with a gun rack.

A truck doesn't have to be new. In fact, the older and more ratty the better. Chronic mechanical difficulties are also acceptable, for they add character.

For instance, E.T.'s old '56 was fast, but it could only move in a straight line. He'd never quite got around to repairing the steering, which meant that his aging pickup required a turning radius of two acres. The brakes were shot as well, which led to inventive stopping methods. To this day half the small towns in Ozark land have parking meters which lean at a 45 degree angle.

Women can share a love of trucks, but the relationship will never be as deep as the man-truck bond. Women are much cleaner than men, and a truck whose floorboard does not include beer cans, cigarette butts, shotgun shells and Ho Ho wrappers feels flat out naked. A foam cup full of dried coffee and spider webs should be wedged on the dash. A windshield crack is mandatory. The radio can't work, except on a scratchy AM station with a 24 hour Paul Harvey format. The cab should smell like dust and sweat and gasoline. The grill should have another bird in it.

E.T. and I made it to Oklahoma City after burning enough petroleum to put a temporary halt to the manufacture of powder blue leisure suits. Eventually, the Ozarks cooled off and we headed back home.

Years later, after bouncing around the world doing God knows what, E.T. returned to the hills, got married, had a kid, and bought himself a ranch. Last I heard, old '56 still resides in his back pasture.

One time, on a visit, he and I cruised into town for a slice of pie at the local diner. It's a friendly little place where E.T. lives, whose hospitality extends to free parking. Of course, I suspect that wasn't the original intent.

For some reason, none of the meters work.

Fear Of Flying

I suppose that man is meant to fly. After all, if he was born with the brains to think up a heavier than air machine, then it would be a shame for all that good skull sweat to go to waste. Birds were obviously meant to take wing because they were born with them. Man was obviously meant to shed his earthly bounds because he was demented enough to come up with idea of sticking a bunch of monster Pratt and Whitney engines on a hollow metal tube and go hurtling through the air at speeds exceeding the sound barrier. Man also came up with stuff like guillotines and Mormonism and hydrogen bombs and Gilligan's Island, which should tell you something right off.

So, for argument's sake, lets just admit that man as a species was meant to defy the hold of gravity. I wasn't.

This creates a problem come the holiday season, for it is the one time of year when I try and get together with family. I live here. They live there. They have a beautiful place and tons of room. I have small square footage and a decor which could best be described as early American tar paper. There's several of them. There's one of me. Mom can cook. I'm into beanie weenies. As the tradition of having beanie weenies and a can of cranberry stuff has yet to become popular. I go there.

This causes stress. I hate stress.

The situation has come up because of a call from Robin the Cortez Colorado Travel Counselor. Robin and I have known each other for something like 10 years now, and for the last five of that she has always called me prior to Christmas to make sure I get a ticket home. She knows that I have a mental block about things like doing laundry and buying airline tickets, and thus has taken on the sacred duty of shattering my ticket procrastination habit. As for the laundry thing, I just wait till people tell me I stink.

Robin called just last week. However, for some reason, this year, I just cannot force myself to step foot on the evil and devious creation of Orville and Wilbur.

This year, come Christmas, I'm driving.

This may sound silly to a lot of people, spending two or three days to get to a place when you could easily arrive in three or four hours, but that's just the way I am. I'd rather throw the wolfhound into the Jimmy and take off across the snow swept plains of Wyoming, face the dastardly blizzards of Montana, than get locked in an airplane. I'd rather carry the sleeping bag and rifle and bottled water and Twinkies and long underwear and electric socks and full complement of Arctic gear and maybe even a flare gun than sit in first class Delta munching old peanuts and tough steak. I'd rather white knuckle it for 1,350 miles—risk driving in a ditch and freezing my feet off like those idiot Stolpa people they made the TV movie about—than worry about dropping out of the sky like a gut shot mallard.

Why? Because I'm stupid, that's why.

Mental wattage notwithstanding, there are a number of reasons I despise the airline demons. Part of it has to do with the fact that I don't enjoy being stuck in small places with people I don't know who probably have the swine flu and want to give it to me. Part of it has to do with the fact that I don't enjoy people I don't know who, just because they are crammed next to me tighter than Cindy Lou on prom night, feel honor bound to engage me in insipid personal conversation while I'm thinking about plummeting to the ground and ending up as hash. Part of it has to do with lay-overs, luggage carousals and crowds. Part of it has to do with having to listen to the fat guy with the turban and eye patch sitting next to me gumming a hunk of chicken with yellow goop on it.

That's a French dish, chicken with yellow goop on it, which is another reason I don't like to fly. All airline employees are surly, which means they must be French, and putting up with their bad attitudes is nasty enough without have to choke down the hog swill they ingest on a daily basis as an integral part of their recommended daily nutritional allowance.

There are many reasons I hate flying, but if we're honest here, there's is one path of logic which supersedes them all.

I'm not the guy flying the plane.

If you want to know the truth, I'm a control freak. I'd rather drive through horrible weather for three days, with me behind the wheel, than sit on a plane piloted by some guy I don't know who is ruminating about either his hangover or the physical attributes of the stewardess slinging drinks in coach. I used to hang out with some commercial pilots in Florida, and the group as a whole did more to scare me away from airline travel than anything on the face of the earth. Most of them were real fond of the phrase "eight hours from bottle to throttle."

This was the pilot guideline as to when the party should stop, since the fly boys had to fire up the 757 in the morning and fly a bunch of orphan children across an ocean or something. Lately, with all the commotion over airline safety, I've heard the new ruling is "12 hours from bottle to throttle," like it makes a difference.

So, this year, with fondest regards to Robin the Cortez Colorado Travel Counselor, I sticking to earth-bound transport. I will not defy the laws of physics. I will not subject myself to the horrors of French people with yellow goop on their lip. I will not get the flu or sit next to international terrorists in training who reek of the boiled goat lung they had for breakfast and feel the urge to badger me to open the window shade so they can face Mecca at 35,000 feet.

I will do as I should have done all along. Robin will understand, she's known me a long time. I'll take a paraphrased lesson from the Greyhound people and leave the driving to me.

Not that I'd ride a bus either. Those things are full of people with hooks and old ladies with shopping carts and religious fanatics and I'm willing to bet there's gum beneath the seats. A bus is only slightly better than a plane, it has a shorter distance to fall, but I'm no fan of that mode of travel either.

You see, I'm not the guy driving the bus.

Climate Is A State Of Mind

I believe it was 1985 when the "No Name Storm" came to town. It was a freak hurricane, a tad small by tropical standards, arising from the Gulf with neither warning nor mercy. It was also my first true encounter with the climate gods.

Armed with Crow the Labrador Retriever, a 1983 Monte Carlo with t-tops and a wandering attitude, I came to the gator filled swamps and elderly filled condos of South Florida in No Name's wake. I adopted a psychotic parrot and searched for Jimmy Buffett. I cut mangos in my backyard, broiled on the beach, and wandered the 10,000 Islands in pursuit of snook, redfish, literary inspiration and tranquillity.

For a time the climate was exotic, I'll give it that, till the skies began to boil once again. The ensuing hurricane hit only me, and soon it was time to go.

I waved good-bye to Margaritaville in '92, beloved Labrador having already split to a better place. The snook, redfish and swamps were becoming ever more scarce, the elderly gators more prevalent. The incorrigible parrot (never harbor a stolen parrot, they have no gratitude) had relieved my right hand of too much flesh. Jimmy Buffett moved to Colorado. Somewhere along the line I almost learned that tranquillity is a process of mind rather than geography. Almost.

One week after my departure, a giant wave swamped Daytona Beach. A few weeks later, Hurricane Andrew dropped by. Going against my nature and sliding into metaphysical musings, I took this as a sign. Maybe I had somehow offended the climate gods. Maybe my penance for misdeeds was meteorological purgatory.

I hid for several months in the Ozarks, canoeing, writing and checking in with Ransom Jack, Psycho Bob, Suzie Q and a number of other long lost friends. Later, I raced for Idaho during a December heat wave. The San Rafael Mountains of Southern Utah leaped from the pages of a Zane Grey novel, cut a hard left through my windshield, and printed indelibly on my mind. It was gorgeous, so pretty I almost forgot I was in that most mentally unbalanced state of the contiguous forty eight. My hope was to locate a new climate, as well as retrieve something lost, or perhaps never found. I kept moving.

The first morning after arriving in southwestern Spud Land, two feet of new snow lay on the ground. The winter was long and fierce. I frantically searched for the meaning of life in a space heater, and was answered with naught but hot air. Idaho was not a place I cared to linger, as I soon discovered that it's capitol was located in Salt Lake City. S.W. Idaho's attitudes were a little perverse for my tastes (I think it may hold the distinction, second only to Utah, of being America's top exporter of the status quo) for it is a land totally unaccepting of individuality or differing opinion. I did linger for a grueling year and a half, true, but only until I could escape with body parts, bank-book and sanity intact. Montana beckoned with a friendly smile, laughing voice, honest acceptance and its unique, one-of-a-kind attitude. My response was "feets don't fail me now. I be headin' north." It was the best decision I ever made.

Soon Montana will get cold again. A friend, knowledgeable in the lore of things weatherwise, tells me that the winter to come could make the North Pole seem like Aruba in July. The squirrels have been acting weird, he proclaims. The migratory birds have already stocked up on

Ray Bans and S.P.F. 40 sun block. Another friend plans to go south for the winter. He says he is at least as smart as a bird. I smile and agree.

But, I don't care. I'm staying here for the snow times. Gladly! Winter is nothing when stacked up against kindness and truth and the marvelous trait of straightforward speech. My boasts of nearly a decade ago that I would never live in a place where the mercury dipped below 70° are now attributed to the stupidity of youth.

The mercury's indolent ambition is not major cause for alarm, but merely something you enjoy and deal with. In matters of climate, a good novel, hot blues, warm conversation and perhaps a bottle of Silverado cabernet serve as dandy equalizers. I've learned but one or two things in my life, the most important being that when the climate god's speak, one best acquiesce.

I no longer feel that the spectral arbiters of the elements are irked at me personally. In retrospect, such notions are pure hubris. Premature infridgidation is random and unfeeling and really not too terribly important. It is graciously unpredictable, and frankly, I've come to like surprises.

Climate is fleet footed. You can't catch it or bind it to your desires. The rumored sunshine beyond the next hill may well be a matter of perception. Searching for the perfect climate is a noble goal, but the quest can lead to exhaustion and frustration. Climate takes on innumerable guises. Appreciate their spontaneity and let it go at that.

Sometimes a storm is required to clear the air, a lightning barrage necessary to improve vision. Whatever, don't take the whims of the climate gods personally, for they have their own agenda.

The same could be said of life itself.

My Dinner With Bud

Bud's Diner was fake plastic planters and green vinyl booths patched with duct tape. It was a social demilitarized zone, a place where diamond draped matriarchs shared counter space with aromatic shrimpers and bleached out dock bums.

Bud's was not owned by anyone named Bud, but rather by an Italian Bostonian named Sammy. The original Bud was long dead, a cherished myth in the annals of chicken friend steak smothered in cream gravy. After his demise a succession of pretenders had attempted to claim the Bud crown, but all were eventually ousted in the greasy spoon version of a bloodless coup. That is, until Sammy came along.

Under Sammy's tutelage, Bud's surpassed its former glory. The chicken fried steak was a joy to behold, the liver and onions a legend. Of course, as always happens, the word soon spread. Bud's was discovered. It became the "in" place. That, was the beginning of the end. Sammy, deciding to cash in on his popularity, finally sold his place to a couple of misguided Yuppies. They transformed Bud's into a art deco bistro that served spinach quiche and low cholesterol eggs. Not being short order people, they went bust in short order.

The moral of the story? If you trip across something great, keep it a secret. By the time a place becomes hip, it's not hip any more. It's just another place.

At least I used to think that. Now I'm not so certain.

Recently I've been eavesdropping on conversations around town. Much moaning is raised over the "newcomers" who flock to the Pacific Northwest. From what I can gather, many locals don't want their pristine area ruined by a rampaging horde of Californians in search of hipness.

My advice? We best learn to lay back and enjoy it. When humans get in the moving binge, there's no stopping their progress.

We're a migratory species with a herd mentality, consistently flocking in droves toward greener pastures. As a relative newcomer to this area myself, I'm probably more sensitive than most to the complaints of encroaching urban devils who clutter the wide skies and forested peaks of the northern Rockies. On the other hand, I understand. I used to say the same things during my Florida days, reciting the litany of "damn tourists, damn Yankees" on a daily basis. I didn't want my beaches packed with the pasty white denizens of Manhattan, didn't feel the Everglades should be despoiled by a bunch of condo crazy Michiganites.

I've been welcomed quite warmly in the northwest, but that's always the case for long haired, hermit writers who can fix exotic rum drinks. Nevertheless, Being on the other side of the migration lends great perspective and sympathy. In Florida, in my arrogance, I forgot that I too had once come from somewhere else. Truth be told, at one time or another, we all did. Unfortunately, the curse of man is that he forgets. We don't always work and play well with others.

Still our desire to belong and enjoy a sense of place and purpose, that home and hearth thing, is a formidable entity. Maybe it's because I'm newly planted. Maybe it's because I've migrated a few too many times and have a tendency to remember. Whatever. When I hear reports of a threatened influx of Californians, Texans, Martians or dog people, I smile. The one thing I've learned, the lesson that came too late in the beach years, is that life and growth are symbiotic, always inspiring new viewpoints and new opportunities.

I really don't think people are scared of newcomers. They're just afraid of change. Change can bring problems, but I'm not so sure that such difficulties aren't less severe than those caused by stagnation. You have to remember, change is not necessarily good and not necessarily bad. It's just different. Besides, it's not like there's a choice in the matter.

Maybe, if we're lucky, one of those Californians will open a decent diner.

Wild Geese

*T*he wild geese have been flying low this past week. They honk and squawk and throw caution to the odd February winds that have turned warm too early. A false spring such as this can be dangerous, much moreso for people who love that plaintive wail than for the geese themselves. The dormant circuit breakers flip to the on position, the voltage crackles down wires not yet ready to wake. For a brief moment, mistaking temporary winter relief for a burst of constant energy, we run too hard and live too fast and quest after those things which our cloudy eyes are not yet ready to see.

The wild geese will no doubt survive when the mercury once again plummets, for they are adept at such things. Those who hear their primordial call may not fare so well.

I am a sucker for the sound of wild geese, both those of the feathered variety and those that fly in my mind. In years past that imagined cry would send me running for the door, and in truth the wild goose has been both the bane and joy of my existence. On the one hand it has been the lure of a far horizon, the anticipation of a new adventure, the unseen smile of an unknown love. On the same token, that piercing scream has often led to crumbling paths and frivolous loss and the acrid smell of burning emotions. Sometimes the goose would soar. Sometimes it would merely cook.

Weeks such as this, I have learned, are the times when I should be bound, shackled, heavily sedated and locked in the root cellar. I become more irrational and cantankerous than usual, am torn between the desire to flee and the need to stay. The old ways bubble to the surface unbidden, and the simplicity which I have carefully constructed comes clattering down around my shoulders. It is a manic time against which walls and armor offer little protection. Contrary to popular belief, fear is not the only thing we have to fear. When the wild goose cries, it is much wiser to fear ourselves. As usual, our most devious adversaries come from inside.

I suppose that this is always the case, but at least for me, the warm days in the cold times bring out the ancient demons in full marching regalia. I no longer succumb totally to their invitations of the blue high-way—there is a small victory in that I enjoy where I am far too well to run from it—however the battle rages nonetheless. Fits of nostalgia and pangs of long ago regret make the old scars ache and old memories beckon. It is a cocktail of heady wine and honey gone sour, all mixed and shaken in the dark and thorny places.

But of course, as I have been told more than few times in my life, this too will pass. One morning soon I will awaken to snow and cold, and the biological instincts of season will allow the internal compass to slow its dervish whirl. All will be normal, or at least as normal as it gets. I will stop worrying about the myriad aspects of the future—quit hovering over my recently sick dog like a mother hen, stop fretting at the check-book's nonexistent balance, avoid questioning my own decisions—and concentrate again on the here and now.

Unlike the low flying geese that mistakenly think towards spring, it is the obligation of man to recognize false promise. Though we try and deny it, our duty is to realize that all things happen in their time, no matter whether or not there is reason. You can't force the river, you can't tame the wind. To even try is to court disaster.

The wild geese are honking again. I peer out the window and see nothing but a cloudy sky. Rationally I recognize that sound as the siren song, a sweet and treacherous melody of my own creation which might lead to rainbow's treasure but would most likely end on shoals of sharpened coral. Maybe I'm just gettin' old. Maybe, as is the way of the world, my needs are changing. Maybe, for once, my love of place has superseded my love of movement.

I pull the shade and retreat to safer harbor. The wolfhound, still a tad delicate but quickly recovering from his bout with pneumonia, looks at me with soulful eyes and offers a touch of a smile. I scratch his ears and wait. I do not know if this is good or bad, but the pull of wild goose tune is a bit less entrancing than before.

But my…isn't it a pretty sound?

Saying Farewell

Buffett the Wolfhound was born on December 12th, 1993. he was an orphan, a foundling whom I took into both home and heart. In my heart, at least, he will always remain.

Though originally from Utah, I rescued the pup at an early enough age that he was spared the traditional Joseph Smithstilian brain-scrubbing. We spent a few brief days in Idaho before heading off to Montana in a horrible blizzard. I got a migraine on that trip. Buff slept the sleep of innocence.

Buff was with me when I started a newspaper. In his early days—before he grew so large as to cause riots and scare horses—he was my constant companion in the Bear Trap Canyon. He comforted me at the deaths of dear relatives and good friends, celebrated in joy when I bought my first house. He treasured my smiles on the day of my one and only marriage, and if he lives another week, will share both steaks and relief on the day of my one and only divorce.

Buffet the Wolfhound was diagnosed with cancer a couple months back. He's already outlived the prognosis and, at the time of this writing, is eating like a horse and playing with my other fur wagons. Thanks to phenomenal vets who have cared for my beloved dog as if he were their own (Mike and Eileen White of Ennis, Montana to be exact) Buffett is happy. While his time is short, and though the thought of that terrible inevitability fills my soul with anguish, his last weeks are being lived as if he were king of the world.

What is it about dogs? Why do some of us prefer the company of canines to the presence of people? Those who do not share a love of wagging tails and barking smiles seem to sneer at the very concept, muttering snide remarks about anthropomorphizing a "dumb animal." They say that devotion to a dog is based upon selfishness, that we love them because they don't talk back.

Cretins who espouse this philosophy are not fully human. At best they are ice-blooded oafs who have spent their lives thinking sentiment is the grit that collects in the pool filter. Waste not your time with their madness, for it will only lead to infuriation.

I'll tell you what it is about dogs. For one thing, most do not have a malicious bone in their body. They are quick with compassion, quicker yet to forgive. They do not plot, scheme, manipulate or lie. They may be devious from time to time,—generally when seeking out a bit of beef left unguarded on the kitchen table—but these actions are not perpetrated with an eye toward betrayal or Machiavellian artifice. It's simply free food.

Anyone who can look in a dog's eyes and fail to see unconditional love should get thee to an optometrist, for blindness has occurred.

On the evolutionary scale, at least emotionally, I would rate most dogs above most people. And, Buffett the Wolfhound lies close to the top of that list. Thirty four inches at the shoulder and 170 pounds in his prime, this was and is the most gentle creature I have yet to encounter. He has been loyal to his family and kind to all that met him. All it took was a single word of encouragement to bring a smile to that saber-tooth set of chompers. All it took was the sound of a rustling trash bag to send him running for cover. He has never been a fighter—Buff would always rather share a plate of cold spaghetti than get in a rumble—but he has always been a friend.

I am tired of writing about death and loss, but it has been a death and loss type of spring. Frankly, there are some magnificent events happening at the same time, but I suppose for right now I wear them close to the chest like secret armor. Still, the only thing that has truly taken me to the depths of despair has been the impending death of my best friend. That's not meant to sound cruel or uncaring, but the other nightmares were inevitable and predictable. In such cases you grieve for a short time, and then go on enjoying your life to the fullest. To do otherwise is to give power to the dark and insane.

But to lose a young dog, a great dog, is an unmatched tragedy.

I guess I should count blessings for the few weeks I have been given in which to say good-bye. It's been sausage, steak and bacon every night, a thousand scratches behind the ears, and long hours of play in the backyard. I will treasure these moments forever, our talks both verbal and silent, but am devastated over the approaching conclusion. It's just not right.

Relish every second. Cherish every smile. Live kindly with grace and honor, for you never know when your life will be a memory. This is how Buffet lived, and I hope I learned from him.

He's looking at me with that big toothy grin.

It's time to play tug-o-war.

Sandhill Spring

*T*he sandhill cranes have returned to the swamp behind my house. Although I've yet to see them dance, leaping and bobbing in the annual sandhill rendition of half-price margarita night at the singles bar, I have heard them talk. That tremulous scream—acappella Tarzan caterwaul mixed with a gullet-full of Listerine—is sorta' hard to miss.

I like the sandhills, look forward to their coming. They remind me that spring is hiding just over the northern Rocky horizon. Their presence reminds me of times when—as a barefoot Missouri boy under a warm "Show Me" sky—I would treble-lip the year's first channel cat on hunk of rotten liver. Though it would be foolhardy to assume we are done with winter this far north—April and May are notorious for big howlers—the sandhill's song is perfect counterpoint to the ghostly hint of green sprouting along the fence line.

The sandhills seem to have shown up a bit early this year, or maybe it's just me that's a bit early. This winter past was tame as a puppy and my frame of reference has gone goofy. El Nino favors the northern climes—the mercury brushed the ten below mark only once or twice—and my time sense is about as accurate as a cheap wristwatch with a drunken mainspring. The second hand is flying 'round the dial—it's been doing that ever since a downright balmy February—and I keep writing the wrong month on my checks.

Now there's a human being for you; I wonder when it was that we lost our indigenous savvy and began relying on clocks, calenders, fortune tellers and The Weather Channel? Perhaps the price our species paid for acquiring a questionably accelerated intellect and opposable thumbs was the dulling of intuition and natural awareness. Perhaps the gift of creativity and imagination was impossible to bestow without the theft of visceral insight.

Perhaps I simply lack the inborn vision to know such stuff.

Naaah…that's just a convenient excuse.

I do believe that a certain sixth sense lies below our overly-cognitive surface, but we're all so busy hurrying, worrying and creating "what if" scenarios that we attribute the mild pangs and elusive feelings to a lack of sleep or a bit of bad beef. I'm not talking about Kreskin shenanigans or the shysters who claim to bend forks with their brains while fleecing the gullible. I'm talking instinct, a corollary to the old concept of birds do it, bees do it, even Dom Delouise do it.

So what about us? Do we really fail to recognize the whispered messengers that rise unbidden dependent upon season and circumstance? They're readily apparent in the fight or flight reflex, the way the neck hairs bristle when being eyeballed by hidden carnivores of either the two or four-legged sort. They're manifest in the actions and attitudes of those increasingly rare folks who possess a semi-functional conscience, evident in the way such people automatically sniff and discard unpalatable behavior as if it was offal in August.

Hell, the unmapped perceptions of biological imperative are even visible to the naked eye. Ever see the way Wisconsin girls bulk up at the onset of winter? I've been to Milwaukee in November. It's frightening.

Actually, it could be that humans and other animals are not that dissimilar. We all eat, sleep and seek shelter from the storm. Critters of the field react without thought, their response to outside stimuli as autonomic as the beating of a heart, their heightened senses compensating for the lack of a logic chip in the skull. The lucky dogs live totally in the present and time is irrelative.

In humans, the analogous capability is called common sense. We basically know the same things, but we think about them first.

Unfortunately, way too many people prefer not to think at all, disregarding sagacity and gut wisdom out of social posturing or sheer irresponsibility. Deep down we know a liar when we hear one, but prefer ignorance & restraint over judgment and truth. We intrinsically realize the difference between good and evil, but hold our tongues least we be called to bear witness, mete out punishment or justify our stance.

We know the answers, but pretend otherwise out of fear of getting our hands dirty. Humans don't lack instinct, they're just lazy. Apathy is easier—accepting the falsely ambivalent mutterings of the self-serving—than trusting one's own brain and soul.

The sandhills are back early this year, at least it seems that way to me. I could sabotage my happiness at their arrival—dwell on ifs and whys and whens—but it would change nothing. The sandhills would still be here. Frankly, I'd rather relish their return than waste time belaboring the obvious.

Thinking is a fine gift, the first step toward greatness. Its power is infinite, but infinitely corrosive when geared towards self-deception.

The sandhills are back—early or not—and spring is on the horizon. This is an inescapable fact.

As is true with most inescapable facts, not much thought is required.

When The Fox Gnaws

*I*t was the beaming smile that came with a churn of hand-cranked ice cream and a glass of homemade lemonade. It was the bottomless laugh that came from watching a young dog jump and bark and tumble aimlessly as he chased a grasshopper through the high weeds. It was the boundless joy which would arise unbidden from the scent of a cool rain hanging over the horizon, from the invisible splash of a bass on a midnight pond, from the glimpse of a crimson sunset on a warm summer's night.

All those things still bring enjoyment, but a good portion of the unbridled enthusiasm of youth seems to become dulled by age, analysis and a totally irrational devotion to the perceptions of others. We guard our emotions and reactions for fear they might be viewed as unseemly or juvenile. We keep silent our thoughts and ideas least a cynical observer deem them silly or irrelevant.

We, as a society, care more about keeping up with the Joneses than with the Jonese's well-being. We are becoming, or maybe have become, or maybe always were, a tribe who worships at the church of the almighty status quo. In our march to have the latest convenience and highest community reputation, we have forgotten those things that are truly important.

Life used to be simple. Life should be simple. The fact that it is not simple is our fault rather than life's. We are too busy being adults. We are, to quote my friend Ransom Jack, seriously humor impaired.

I've never truly understood why adults seem totally baffled by the ways of children. If I'm not mistaken, most adults were once children themselves. Is the memory so faulty they forget the eyeblink that was yesterday? Why is it so difficult to recall a belief in magic, to revel in the happiness of simply being happy, or feel a depth of sadness over a dropped ice cream cone or lost pup? Does responsibility and age invariably equal ennui and impatience, or do we simply get old and surly and set in our ways?

Don't ask me, for I'm doing this whole trip backwards.

I was one of those serious kids, one who had an ulcer by age eight and stewed upon the expectations of damn near everybody. Luckily, and unlike many people I know, I was blessed with incredible parents who made life at home a joy. However, when off the confines of our farm, away from the trees, fields, fishing holes and beagles, I transformed into a miniature adult. The world confused me back then. I found it daunting and dangerous and fraught with worry and concern.

The world still confuses me. I still think it's dangerous, but that comes mostly from the times we live in, our sordid government and the actions of the ever-growing population of miscreants with zero concern for life or property. Worry and concern still linger, but are somewhat negligible.

Yes, I'm consistently stunned at the antics of society, but mostly I'm just amused.

I'm also selfish, which is why I do pretty much what I please. I like this life, and plan to get as much out of it as possible. Shoot me...I'm having fun. At some point I discovered that life is too short for worry and too long for shackles.

The fact of the matter is that it's all too easy to get revved up over government, religion, the latest health scare, the ozone layer, political correctness or the highly publicized babblings of some loud-mouthed Yahoo (including this loud-mouthed Yahoo) whose opinions receive more than passing notice. These things don't mean squat. You have to keep a sense of humor about them, for most opinions are (or should be) like rain on a rock. If you don't like them they should just bounce off. If you want to remember them, catch a few drops in a glass for later consumption. The important thing is to keep laughing. As Robert Heinlein once said, "when the fox gnaws....smile!"

Simplicity may not come to those who wait, but it does come to those who seek it. I've noticed that the people who are happiest are those that take it all in, say what they think and move on to the next day. They have the time and ability to enjoy stuff like hand-cranked churns of ice cream, good conversation and real friends. They can chuckle as the fish splash, giggle at the silly pup and feel their jaw drop as the first shimmering beams of sunrise blaze forth from Olympus. They have the advantage of a child's outlook and an adult's experience. They know that the little things count most.

Maybe the key to a fine life lies in remembering what fun it is to laugh Or maybe more important, what to laugh at.

Beyond The Rainbows

She was born in the same year as Rudolph Valentino and Babe Ruth, was nearly eight when the Wright Brothers launched their first kite from the sandy hills of Kitty Hawk.

She was 30 by the time Clarence Darrow and William Jennings Bryant argued monkey evolution in a smoky Tennessee courtroom, had turned 46 before the Japanese bombed Pearl Harbor. On that sultry July night when Neil Armstrong made his small step for man, she no doubt pondered the 74 years between horse-drawn cart and travel to the stars. Her husband had long since passed, but she was full of happiness with her cows and chickens, friends and family.

Life is all perspective, a blazing fuse which flares brightly and departs. It is uncaring and cruel, yet the tumultuous wake of its apathetic voyage provides infinite laughter. It is success and failure, tragedy and defeat. Often, it is sad. Often, it is not.

Life, I guess, is what you make of it. My Grandmother, who now lays dying at 102 years of age, made more of it than most.

Her's is a story worth telling, however it seems best to avoid the lingering final chapter. That epilogue is not consistent with the rest of the book. I do not wish to delve deeply into the tortures that occur when one's mind and spirit exceed the warranty on their body, but having seen it before, cannot elude the reality.

So, though I cannot imagine the pain of her ordeal, I strive to remember her in a different way. It is easy for me to recall the good times, for they are forefront in my mind.

I watch myself as a small child, riding my bike down the gravel road to her house. Every day, or so it seemed, I would take a nasty spill over the mud-hole at her driveway entrance. Tears flowing from my eyes, she was always there with kind words and soothing hands.

I recall us kids, my brother, self and the neighbor boys, finding scraps of lumber and constructing a makeshift clubhouse in the backyard. I can feel the games of hide and seek with my cousins, the demise of many a egg-stealing blacksnake with hoe and corn knife. I can taste the cold water she pumped from the old well, the noodles in tomato sauce she laid upon the table. I can smell the acrid stench of wet feathers on the day we plucked the chickens.

I can hear the big bell in the backyard, her laughter at Archie Bunker and the soft warnings to avoid the skunks which had taken up residence in the ramshackle garage.

She taught me to fish, informing me it was better to sit on the bank and enjoy the day ("just as cheap," she'd say with a smile) than to expend great effort chasing the wily bluegill. She taught me to bind my pocketknife to a long stick, and grinned as I gigged frogs for our supper.

My beagles and I lived in her hay barn, building castles and dreams while keeping a wary eye for evil serpents. Her old collie, Trixie, hovered always near, reminiscing over the days when she too leapt from bale to bale.

I could tell you stories of the hard times Grandma endured, but not here. They are important, but the real story is her appreciation of life.

She was quick with a needle, her quilts a thing of sheer beauty. She knew the importance of dogs, loving them one and all with a fervor passed on to me. She was guardian, teacher and friend to her children and grandchildren, always ready for an adventure. No matter if it was a walk to the pond, a blackberry pick in her beloved Prosperity woods or a trip through the pasture under rusted barbed wire. She was game.

My Grandmother will leave us very soon. Though our hearts will cry with her passing, though a part of us will shiver and die, she will live on through our thoughts and actions.

I will always see her at age 90, the day I left for far southern lands. She was wearing her old straw hat with the green visor, carrying an ax on the way to chop down a tree that obstructed her view. I will remember her keen mind, razor sharp despite the protests of her body. I will remember her love.

Grandma's face came alive at the sight of a rainbow. She knew the unequaled joy of both sunset and sunrise. She understood that such things were important, not to be taken for granted, and in turn gave her family the awareness of their importance.

In her final sunset, I will try and remember her gifts.

I will remember visions of dogs and frogs, caring and kindness.

And maybe, somehow, I will look at a rainbow and remember to smile.

Prophets Versus Profits

*O*ur earth is degenerate in these latter days; there are signs that the world is speedily coming to an end. Bribery and corruption are common, children no longer obey their parents, every man wants to write a book and the end of the world is evidently approaching.

Think I'm a doomsday prophet? Think I'm a right-wing radical obsessed with traditional values? Think I'm about ready to strap on the M-16, zip the Kevlar and join the Montana militia? Think that the cynical, hermit boy of the Tobacco Roots has finally tripped over the precipice of Republican reality?

Think again. I may well be all, some or none of those things, but the above words aren't mine. Actually they were uttered several years before my time—about 4,796 years to be exact. That dunning admonition of a corrupt and declining society bereft of courtesy and grace was discovered on an Assyrian stone tablet carbon-dated to the year 2800 BC.

In short, the more things change...

I suppose it is man's nature to assume himself unique from his predecessors in both thought and deed, to consider himself light years removed in both social and mental evolution from his early ancestors, to self-judge his grandiose concepts as original.

Such is the height of arrogance. While man sporadically evolves at terrifying speeds in terms of technological achievement, his rate of emotional maturation is positively geologic. My bet would be that the human approach to social dynamics and interpersonal relationships was basically the same in the era of Matthew, Mark, Beowulf or Plato as now. We laugh, we cry, we envy, we fight. We covet, we whisper, we gossip, we steal. We do great deeds and perform abominable acts, think great thoughts and act without thinking. Stephen King read Mark Twain who read William Shakespeare who read Homer who heard common myths of vice and virtue, heros and villains passed down from time immemorial. We are none of us archetypical models, we are the collective wisdom and foolishness of untold generations.

Damn…we're merely human…who woulda' thunk it?

The only difference between us present and them past may be that them had more realistic logic in terms of adjudication. It's a survival thing. When life depended on a treasured cache of mastodon blubber, it only made sense to gut those who would steal it from your offspring's mouths. The same concept came into play more recently during the Yukon gold rush. Stores of supplies left in the open remained undisturbed by all but their owner. These things—pick, bedroll, jerky, girlie magazines or whatever—meant life or death in a harsh and unforgiving environment. The silent laws of an invisible community of hardened prospectors stated that to steal a man's life was to forfeit your own.

We, on the other hand, have little worry of survival. Our problems mostly revolve around image, status, fear of change or perhaps one-upping our adversaries. It's fun to bitch about political battles, it's a gas to rage at the heavens over philosophical difference, but in the long run we have it so easy as to be laughable.

Technology giveth and technology taketh away. We gain ease, medical miracles, spare tires 'round the middle and 423 channels with nothing to watch. We lose, I think, a certain appreciation for the importance of life as it was meant to be lived.

I enjoy ranting about politics and our president's shenanigans, but in truth the Machiavellian lawgivers of now are no different than thousands of feudal lords, power mad Cardinals and the well-dressed Neanderthal with the biggest spear. I thrive on abusing the politically correct, the whiny sub-cultures who consider themselves and their problems unique. Still, they are indistinguishable from the jesters, revolutionaries and rabble rousers of hundreds of ages in hundreds of times. They come, they go and this too will pass.

Make no mistake, I deplore a nihilistic approach to life. Ideas are important, people are important, values are important. I think maybe it is the ability to feel anger, outrage and passion—to forget our redundancy in light of the knowledge that history travels a Mobius strip—that defines humanity. I frankly believe that, if man didn't walk the earth, the statistical probability of his creation would surpass calculation. We exist to strive, quest, fight, love and hate. Cool.

But I still find the whole game rather funny, and I still laugh loudly. Like everyone, I have my own faults, foibles, standards of propriety and order of importance.

I caught a 22 inch brown trout last night. It lunged and fought and stripped screaming line from the reel's smoking drag. For a moment I forgot everything but the immediate, the bend of the rod and the adrenaline of the fight. Some things matter…some things don't.

That fish—alive and fine and beautiful—mattered far more to me than most events or concerns, and mattered infinitely more than childish modern grumblings. It wasn't the catching nor the eating. It was the sensation, the exhilaration, the blood-tumbling rush.

That's not an original thought. Not even close.

But, luckily, it always feels that way.

Atlantis Revisited

*T*he water dripped off the limestone cliffs, a gravity-driven chamber group which filled the hidden Ozark meadow with a deep forest symphony of minor chords and off-key rhythms. This was a good day in a good land—south Missouri rarely hits the 65° mark in late December—and I had been gone for a too long time.

The trunks of the elderly cottonwoods were gnawed and thin, ready to fall with the first bad wind or second good shove. The beavers had obviously been eating well, a point further emphasized by the stripped branches littering the bed of a crystal creek which, by all rights, should not have existed.

And that's what most caught my eye and imagination. Barely a quarter mile long, this ribbon of sleeping water appeared to have no source and no outlet. Still, there it was, lined with caves, crevices and a blue hole the depths of which I could not conjecture. Most of the creek—I'd guess—was of the subterranean variety, and I had but stumbled across the tiny part that surfaced for air before once again sounding to the far reaches of the great abyss. On the other hand, I didn't give the physics of the matter all that much thought. The concept of a place with no end and no beginning was a little too seductive to avoid.

For some reason this particular stretch of the Ozarks consistently provides me with an influx of energy and a case of the giggles. Though neither as awesome nor mysterious as my Tobacco Root Mountains, it holds a nature that is both courteous and violent. It is a place where cynical humor and pragmatic hilarity are the rule, a place holding a vivid aversion to—and blatant disregard of—rules and laws that defy common sense. It is a place still civilized due to its lack of mass civilization, a place where the complaining and ultra-sensitive are viewed with polite mocking and not so polite commentary. It is a place of rugged individuality—a slim harvest in rocky soil—where the ability to persevere in the face of life's hardest blows confers far greater respect than the ability to whine, blame or pout.

It's a lot like Montana, only shorter.

No ending and no beginning; it might be good theory for little Ozark creeks with nary a care in the world, but it's a crummy philosophy for we human types. Unfortunately such is the way too many folks live their lives and too many governments approach their policies and practices. There is a fine and elusive art in living day to day, enjoying the little things like smelly dogs and a whiplash blizzard, while at the same time following a vaguely certain grand scheme.

The art consists of hoping for the best but not being surprised by the worst, standing your ground with the bending strength of the willow and the stubbornness of a mule. It entails seeking the humor in all things, ignoring the knee-jerk reactions of those eminently serious individuals who neither think, listen nor see clearly, and attempting to find laughter in even the most dire of circumstances. It involves a combination of learned indifference with firm resolve, centering around a conviction that the opinions of others need not intrude upon your existence. It is the status bestowed by George Carlin—"if you're part of the solution, you are the problem"—in regard to those who would sully your day by obtrusive whimpering over the inherent unfairness of life.

Mostly, the art is about knowing your own mind. It's main tenet lies in realizing that romance, adventure, success, or whatever must be partially created by those who seek it. It also lies in realizing that such things will have an end, not to mention a middle, chock full of both the good and bad sort of surprises.

I left the Ozarks a happier soul and returned to the house at Tarpaper Acre. I understood that though the pretty little creek might seemingly have no end and no beginning, its surface appearance was merely one junction in a long journey. It had miles to go before it slept, and the whims of observers mattered to it not a whit. I remembered that I'd been at many places and points on the map as well—sometimes in stagnation, sometimes in stampede—yet through it all there was a hovering dream full of starts, stops and twists of face.

I've seen the beginning. Right now I'm in the middle. Some day there will be an end. I think, for best results, you do what you can and you do it well. No regrets and no complaints.

Enjoy the sleepy creeks, for they're mighty pretty. Just remember that sooner or later sleepy creeks always become rapids.

And, assuming they don't kill you, rapids can be a whole lot of fun.

Look But Don't Touch

*T*he Devil's Icebox was a fine place, a wilderness area containing all sorts of rock bridges, underground rivers, bat-filled caves and bottomless sinkholes. Crow the Labrador and self lived next door to the Icebox and visited near daily. The Forest Rangers knew Crow on a first name basis, they knew me as the guy with the labrador. They gave him dog biscuits, they gave me leeway to meander as I pleased. It was a nice arrangement. I won't mess up your playground, you don't meddle in my plans.

I was much younger in those days, less cynical about the nature of man, and always ready to follow a good dog. We waded the creeks during a flood that smashed every footbridge to smithereens. I still have the fossils, arrowheads, spear point and saber-tooth fang that washed up from the depths. We prowled the dripping caves. I still have the photo of him, eyes red from the K-Mart flash, retrieving a water-soaked branch from an underground pool. We played Frisbee in the meadows, inspected beaver dams and rarely saw a half dozen souls over a full weekend. Those folks we did see ignored us as we ignored them, for the Icebox was a place geared to wandering your own mind as much as wandering the deer-paths and mud-slick trails.

I didn't see The Devil's Icebox for a decade, moving off to a far-away land. Time slips away and—at least for a few of those years—I came to believe that a traditional life was what society demanded. That dementia passed quickly—the only use I saw in a station wagon was to enter it in a demolition derby, the only reason I saw for a wife was to share the workload when it came time to fill out divorce papers. The idea of settling down did and does equivocate in my mind to lying still under six feet of dirt. It was time to go.

Crow died at 6:00 p.m. on June 8th, 1992. I quit the job and dodged the bullets of the woman seeking unholy matrimony. Within a week I was back on the road.

Call it a sense of duty, my last salute to an old friend, but the first place I traveled was The Devil's Icebox. I wanted to say my good-byes in a place of hope and happiness, not on a regulated beach surrounded by fat New Yorkers and screeching boom-boxes. I imagined a short and tearful farewell.

I was wrong. The Icebox as I knew it had vanished.

The more things change, the more they stay changed. The wild paths were now lined with hand rails and "keep off the grass" signs. Climbing was prohibited due to liability concerns. The grotto under the giant rock-bridge was blockaded with wire, and I'm pretty sure the authorities would have drawn, quartered and prosecuted anyone who tried to explore a sinkhole. The haven of my youth had become a strictly managed tourist attraction. Look but don't touch. See but don't enjoy. Imagine but don't act.

I could almost hear the pieces of my heart clanking upon the asphalt as I read one final sign. Dogs were not allowed.

I think about the Icebox now and again, the dangerous beauty of it's early days compared to the funereal appearance deemed appropriate for stupid citizens by government protectors. It reminds me of Yellowstone, now only a poorly managed zoo, a vestigial memory of its once proud self. It reminds me of America, a country built on rugged individualism that placed the will of the individual far above the wishes of dictatorial government bodies. Our leaders were once patriots, now they are traitors who rent the White House by the hour, treating the Lincoln Bedroom as if it were a combat zone bordello.

Few of us complain. Fewer seem to care. We place our destiny in the fumbling hands of the incompetent

Look but don't touch. See but don't enjoy. Imagine but don't act.

So, I look at the mountains out my window, still wild but getting less so all the time, and realize that "keep off the grass" signs are becoming more prevalent. I touch the picture of the Labrador and gaze at the wolfhound. It is nice to know there are some constants in life.

I imagine wild places hidden from those who would destroy fun and beauty least we laugh too much or enjoy too long. Our "civilized leaders"—and their complacent followers—are already interfering with those of us in the highlands, frequently demanding compliance with their ways and thoughts. Unable to control their own pitiful lives, they wish to control ours with laws, restrictions and bans. Unfortunately, fighting them is like fighting smoke, for the enemy is the apathy of an entire nation. Changes are seeping through the cracks, and I hate them.

As with The Devil's Icebox, some changes are simply to hideous to be borne. I suspect that someday I will have to act, to walk off towards deep woods and never look back.

On that day a labrador will smile.

Testing Your Meddle

I was scanning the papers and TV stations this morning, hoping against hope something witty and amusing was going on in the world. I read about Saddam Hussein, heard about terrorists in Egypt and perused the tale of giant, vegetarian rats that have run amuck in South Florida.

I threw down the paper, convinced once again there is nothing new under the sun.

Then, just as I was about to seek inspiration in Dreamland, a CNN moderator began a segment concerning politicians in heated debate over whether or not to provide "on-off" switches for automobile airbags.

More political blather, I thought with disgust. If we want to put "on-off" switches on airbags we should start in the halls of Congress. If people want to risk whacking themselves by not wearing seatbelts or taking advantage of airbags it should be their business, not that of a bureaucracy compelled to meddle in personal affairs. We all have minds; we don't need pork-hungry, power-freaks mandating legislation designed to protect ourselves against ourselves.

Then it hit me. Maybe the carpet-bagging meddlers on Capitol Hill are the reflection in the pool, a mirror image of the meddling human condition.

To be frank, I truly believe that overt meddling in someone else's particulars is the major cause of humanity's ills. I'd guess that about two thirds of the hideous actions and bothersome occurrences in recorded history were caused by someone who became outraged when the sheep didn't listen and get in line. They fail to understand that a lot of us surly folks just don't like being told what to do, feel our own brains work just dandy.

War, taxes, ridiculous laws, domestic disputes, union tomfoolery, victimless crimes…most of this stuff originates with people who, although they may not want your share of the pie, do intend to tell you how many times you should chew it. The ability to feel slighted at the thought of any unfulfilled whim, and in fact blame the lack of fulfillment on those who ignore the unwanted criticism, is so commonplace that it is even the preeminent focus of our collective humor.

It's everything from the satiric caricature of nagging wives and slacker husbands to dictatorial managers and nosy neighbors. It's Archie demeaning Edith. It's Lucy conning Ricky. It's Dilbert to Dallas to Dangerfield to Democrats. Maybe we laugh because it's so pathetic, and so patently true.

Meddling—insisting you know what is best for another—is the direct cause of every religious jihad ever fought, not to mention the bedrock of the liberal bully-pulpit. It is the theory that, since others are more stupid than us, they must be force-fed unpalatable ideals rather than being allowed to seek success or failure by their own efforts. It is the calamity borne by the Incas, the Saracens (who were cool enough to come back and kick Crusader butt) the Mayans, American Indian tribes (who did it to each other before we did it to them) and every indigenous group who has had the bad luck to come up against a superior power with an attitude. It's a bunch of hooey, albeit the preferred hooey of homo sapiens.

In a logical world (and trust me, that ain't this one) there is but a single instance in which an individual, church, activist group or government has the right to interfere. This scenario—obviously—is when a body asks for direct input. Such phrases as "missionary zeal," "raising awareness" or "social enlightenment" are usually the buzz words of the control freak and—let's face it—we're all control freaks regardless of political stance or social ideology. There are scant few who do not desire to impose their will—intentionally or otherwise—where its not wanted.

Meddling is really no different on a day-to-day level than in the large scale. The humiliating harangues delivered by unsatisfied Little League fathers or frustrated stage mothers to struggling progeny who are doing their level best, the guilt trips, harsh words and sad looks hurled by snapping couples whose partners behave with perceived inappropriateness…these overbearing actions are merely a symptom of dissatisfaction with self or surroundings, an attempt to improve on unhappy circumstance by dictating to others.

The mantra du jour? "Don't be yourself…be what I tell you to be."

In others words, "I know best!"

Sad stuff. "Live and let live" is not a bad credo, however we generally opt for a "live as I say and maybe I'll let you live" approach. The multitudes don't understand the principle that, as long as you shut up about it, you can do damn near anything you want. Government to government or person to person, the world would get along quite nicely if its inhabitants would learn to hold silent (until asked) their opinions on how others should speak, think, or act.

Do I follow my own advice? Hell no. You see, I present my uninvited two bits because I feel they are more correct than the viewpoints of my adversaries.

Funny, that's the exact same excuse my adversaries use.

How can they be so wrong?

Zephyr Reunion

*T*he sky was the color of old lead, a razor-edged rectangle which slid across the peaks of the Madison Range on tracks well slicked by a buckshot veneer of invisible rain and stinging hail. The dull gray sheet stretched beyond sight, racing with sails unfurled before a wicked sirocco born of desert and sea.

No mere gale, the ravenous appetite of this southeaster seemed to inhale all in its heavenly path—low flying clouds, fog and mists levitating towards the seat of the moon in an atmospheric Electrolux. Now you see them, now you don't. For just a moment, I saw.

It lasted either five seconds or an eternity, I'm not sure which. The whistling void, now laid bare by negative ions and primordial magic, became a spectacle of light and diamonds. Mountain passes I've viewed a thousand times before were awash in depth and detail. Somehow, I assume, the firmament played a trick and polished the lens, for untold miles suddenly achieved sparkling clarity. The door opened and new peaks—new to me anyway—sprung from the earth, their cumulus gown ripped away in an Aeolian interpretation of the dance of the seven veils.

Pay no attention to that man behind the curtain, the Wizard's words to Dorothy and Toto popped into my head. Too late, I responded, for we've caught a glimpse of the treasure behind the velvet.

I'd not seen this before, the only vision vaguely similar involved a magnetized blackness which streamed past with whipshot speed in the hours before a southern Gulf hurricane. This was much better than that, for these screaming and irresistible Montana winds were engaged in elemental combat with sage and immovable granite. This gladiator fought with honor, seeking a worthy opponent of equal strength, whereas hurricanes, being a cheap and bullying sort of blow, prefer to pick on tin roofs, trailer parks and lawn furniture.

I watched the storm, a small part of my head poking the edges of questions covering the spectrum of power and weakness, truth and illusion. Mostly though, for the first time in a long time, I felt the nervous chill of wonder. I wondered at the miracle, and at the same time, wondered at how we've lost our faith in miracles.

The early Greeks would have viewed this event with shimmers and shakes, perhaps pondering upon whether the divine caretakers of such things—Boreas, Zephyr, Notus and Eurus—had shirked their responsibilities due to involvement in the Olympian equivalent of a floating crap game. The followers of Zeus and Company would have sacrificed goats, poured libations, danced naked and fallen to their knees. A hefty percentage of us would probably shrug shoulders and turn on the TV, maybe pouring the coal to barely enough curiosity that we hitch up our gumption and flip the satellite toward the Weather Channel.

Technological achievement is a fine thing, but what a shame that it tends to breed cynicism and apathy. Are we so enamored with our own sense of self importance and scientific hubris—our computers, movies, televisions and other reasonable facsimiles of existence—that we prefer the imitation over the actual? It's bad enough to be a tribe of observers, but isn't choosing to observe apery over the authentic a tad morbid?

Don't ask me. I'm as guilty as the next guy—for episodic culpability is as felonious as the consistent version. True, my jaw did bang the floor. Honest, I did stand outside with a goofy and glazed demeanor as tiny shards of ice pelted unknowing bare arms. On the other hand, a part of me wished for—and sorely lacked—that imposing dread which compliments wonder so well.

I hope this isn't true, but in a time when most of our revelations are carefully packaged by Disney and provided free with every Big Mac purchase, maybe the concept of amazement is antiquated. Maybe revelations ain't what they used to be Where are the dragons and chariots, for cryin' out loud? What happened to the gunslingers and pirates? Are they gone forever? Did they walk away in tears at the frightening conjecture that they can't compete with sit-coms, talk shows and the virtual reality of a Microsoft world?

But, for a few seconds there, the fates bestowed a smile in my direction. For a scant moment I was blessed with feelings of old astonishment which I will savor, relish and hopefully retain. They announced that wonder exists, that amazement is real. Believe that in your heart and you're on your way

The vision flashed one last time and was gone in a blink. The door closed, the world was foggy slate and nought but the breeze remained. I felt a wet nose bump my back, scratched canine ears, and returned to what was before.

Still, this latest act in the cosmic play had taken up residency in my soul. It's a prodigal tenant whose unannounced appearance I welcome. Self-imprisoned by unthinking ambivalence in the astonishingly trivial yet surprisingly impregnable maelstrom of modern thought, I'd not even realized its absence.

Sometimes you don't know what you've lost until its gone.

Sometimes you don't know something is gone unless it comes back.

Thanksgiving Done Solo

I have spent Thanksgiving on a white sand beach, steaks sizzling over an open fire and the reggae sounds of Bob Marley sailing on the breeze. The rum flowed and the friends laughed, sending up a woozy toast to our fortune when the dazzling fireball slipped silently into the steaming blue waters of the Gulf.

I have spent Thanksgiving with my family in southern Missouri, a traditional turkey and football extravaganza complete with the sounds of Mom in the kitchen and Dad snoring in the Lazy Boy. The day is slow and lazy, filled to the brim with the treasured scents of home and home cooking. The conversation is easy and the red jello is specked with bananas. The pace is familiar and the atmosphere warm.

I have spent Thanksgiving on the road, stopping into a highway diner for a hunk of pressed turkey loaf, canned gravy and conversation with a hard-dyed waitress attached to the end of a smoldering Marlboro. I have spent Thanksgiving with both an aged labrador and a young wolfhound, all smiles and laughter despite—or maybe because of—a state of wandering poverty. I have spent Thanksgiving alone with a bottle of Wild Turkey, words spilling onto a screen as I record a migrant nostalgic thought. I have spent Thanksgiving in blizzards, in crowds, in love and insane.

Maybe those last two are synonymous, but you get the basic idea. I always remember my Thanksgivings. It is one of our better American holidays in that it is without great expectation. One does not stew over the purchase of an appropriate Thanksgiving gift. A body is not pressured to put on the big show that our commercially perverted holidays—like Christmas—seem to these days require.

If there is any stipulation regarding Thanksgiving, which I doubt, it lies simply in taking a moment to reflect upon the good things of the past year. Our successes seem brighter on this day. Our failures seem more distant. The only sense of competition is for the softest chair, longest nap or last piece of pecan pie.

I've tended, in recent years, to spend Thanksgiving in an untraditional manner. Many think it mandatory to be surrounded by people on this particular Thursday in November. Such is fine if done of free will, however it is not the celebration I choose. I receive many invitations, some which tempt me sorely, however I generally prefer to be a unicycle rather than a fifth wheel. Some folks send invites because they care deeply. Some ask me over because they are kind and decent to the bone. I suspect a couple request my presence because they feel it socially/politically advantageous in the eyes of their neighbors to appear altruistic and benevolent.

No, I tend to celebrate solo, maybe roasting a bird for self and a steak for dog. I may take a drive into the woods—weather permitting—or I might take a stroll through the canyon. I will make phone calls to those both near and far that are in my thoughts and, if the mood strikes, watch the gridiron behemoths engage in their metaphoric massacre. I will miss my family, and at the same time be thankful they are close to me in ways beyond geography. At some point I will remember that family is not necessarily confined to blood relatives, and I will smile.

I will be a lot of things, mostly happy, but what I won't be is isolated in heart or mind. The best part about choosing a somewhat hermitish path is that you come to realize that being by yourself is far different from being alone.

I remember last year's Thanksgiving, a windy day spent eating chili dogs and tater tots with a southern girl I was dating. We watched the

Cowboys whomp the Chiefs and later—as sometimes happens on holidays—engaged in a hellaciously wicked and bizarre verbal joust. That was our last real conversation, and to be honest, I've never been quite certain whether to be thankful for that or not. My gut impression is that we should both be thankful, for those of molten temperament do not function well together in confined spaces and unventilated areas. Volcanic eruptions are pretty, but take a backseat to new sunrises over unexplored mountains.

This year is different. I've had a pretty wonderful 12 months, and things continue to become brighter despite my insatiable need to fiddle with things unbroken. I'll remember this Thanksgiving in the same odd way I remember all the others, not because of infinite feasts or a TV parade complete with the insipid babblings of Katie Couric and an inflated woodpecker, but because I consider myself damned lucky to be in a place that I adore, doing the thing I love best. There could really be nothing better.

Well, The Chiefs might win, but there's no need to push my luck by requesting a miracle.

Tastes Of Spring

*T*he almanac and the weatherman tell me that spring has officially arrived, which just goes to show that neither almanac writers nor meteorologists ever visit the Northern Rockies. True, the days will get longer. Yes, you may see a few bluebirds or the occasional swan. Perhaps, with luck, the mercury might even hit 60° degrees for a few minutes. Still, I know that until sometime around mid-June we can most likely as not awake to several inches of white stuff and a cold northern blow.

The easiest way to define spring in my part of world is to watch for the influx of tourists. They never show up until assured of warm weather. I guess tourists are a little like the swallows returning to Capistrano, with the difference being that swallows don't try and impress you with their $2,000 fly fishing outfits or ask inane questions such as "what time of year do the elk turn into moose?"

Nevertheless, tourists notwithstanding, the thought of spring still strikes a warm chord after a bitter winter such as the one almost past. It hits a little closer to home this year, as spring cleaning has taken on a whole new meaning. Usually, when the sandhill cranes begin their dance, when one can walk outside without fear of freezing off ancillary body parts, I am compelled to brush off the furniture and air out the dog. This year, it's something different entirely. I've recently been compelled to dig through rotting cardboard boxes and broken milk crates in a near frantic need to dispose of my past. Old writings, clothes that seem to have shrunk, unknown photos and a cornucopia of knick knacks, doo dads, gee gaws and jim cracks have become either one with the dump or the Salvation Army.

Don't get me wrong; the important items of years gone by will remain. Heartfelt letters from family and friends, pictures of dogs, old loves, surrealistic sunsets, and critical items such as my bamboo saxophone stay with me forever. It's the unnecessary and little-used that gets tossed. It is the garbage symbolic of a cluttered past that goes up in smoke. I've come to believe the old Chinese adage that the ancient monk was never truly happy until he gave away his rice bowl. The analogy, I think, has not as much to do with possessions themselves as it does with being encumbered by yesterday.

This one way trip to the mental and physical dumpster is in part derived from the fact that—though I swore I would never do this—I've recently purchased the infamous tar-paper shack of McAllister, Montana. This is an ancient house, the original home of Mr. McAllister after whom our wide spot in the road is named. At various times over the years it has served as family home, post office and general store. It is full of history (and a few bats) with next door neighbors that include badger, deer, bear and innumerable other critters. It is weathered and in need of great repair, much as I was when I came to this valley. Looking up at 11,000 foot peaks and down at the Bear Trap Canyon. I feel that, though it has a rich past which will always linger as mental souvenir, it needs a present and a future.

And, as I sorted through my stored belongings in preparation for the impending move, it seemed that so did I.

We all travel with baggage, and the boxes and loose ends eventually not only reach the closet ceiling but also pour over the eaves of the soul. Some things should be kept, some should be cherished, and some should be allowed to sail away on the breeze. The idea is to break a trail for new ideas and experiences, to remember the old ways, to learn from mistakes, and to throw wide the doors to the endless horizon of infinite possibility. You can't do that when barricaded behind the losses and acquisitions which have come before. For one to understand and appreciate today, one must prepare a space for tomorrow.

All things old are new again. Such is a truism, but only if we allow it. With a glad heart I say good-bye to bits and pieces of my past which have outlived their time. They have made me what I am, good or bad, but their day is done.

As the tar-paper shack begins a slow transformation, I hear it's old logs and beaten floors take a breath of new life. As I clean my yesterdays, I inhale deeply as well. The taste is sweet and fresh and new, which is how it should be.

It is the taste of spring.

Tarpaper Acre

*T*hey say that a man's home is his castle. While this statement is especially valid in reference to prissy and inbred members of British nobility, or anybody else who can afford a moat, it also holds grains of truth for all who are demented or humorous enough to purchase ancient property of their very own. While it may be a truism that a man's home his castle, it also seems to be a physical theorem that not all castles are created equal.

Equal? From what I can see a lot of them aren't even created square.

Like their drawbridge bedecked cousins, most old homes are messy and dark with Jurrasic cobwebs hanging over the fridge and a bunch of Banquet TV dinner thingies sitting in the overflowing sink. Many of them are crumbling relics of another time and another place, kind of like their owners. They are structures that make strange, vaguely disturbing intestinal noises as gravity settles them into the Earth, again kind of like their owners.

If an old house were a person it would be a grandfatherly spinner of nostalgia with an unquenchable addiction to refried bean sandwiches and Diet Fresca with a splash of Tequila. A guy with a heart the size of Sri Lanka who spends his days as a Lazy Boy test pilot and his nights as a dreamer. An old fellow with twinkling eyes who believes in life, liberty and the pursuit of legal age co-eds.

Oh, did I mention that as of this afternoon I am officially in the old home/castle business, the proud owner of a little chunk of McAllister, Montana?

Indeed... after several months of legal work, title searches and checking to see if the roof would collapse when I had my dog jump up and down on it to the refrain of numerous James Brown tunes, I have finally gained proprietorship of the manor that I lovingly refer to as Tarpaper Acre. I have achieved the American dream...I am in debt up to my eyeballs. The hermit has an official home where the deer and the antelope play...just like Ted Kaczynsky.

Actually, I have been quite fond of this old place for a couple of years now. From what I am told it is pretty much the original house in the neighborhood, built by Mr. McAllister his own self sometime before the turn of the century. Over the years it has grown and stretched and acquired various appendages, with appendages in this case being defined as no less than three granaries that got nailed onto the place and decided they were rooms. The original structure has ten inch thick logs for walls, which I swear could withstand the blast of the smallish style thermonuclear devices preferred by smelly, lower echelon European members of the atomic community such as France. It has layers of broken siding and bottomless strata of shingles deep enough to give a Trojan archaeologist the screaming willies. It has oodles and oodles of tarpaper. It has been a post office, general store and home to innumerable families.

Frankly, I love it.

You see, aside from the odd manner in which the history of Tarpaper Acre gets a former historian such as your's truly all goo goo eyed, this old place has been the sight of some very fine memories in a very short period of time. The last owner, a good friend and fishing buddy who was bushwhacked by the Big C almost a year ago, did a great semiremodeling job before he shed this mortal coil. I've spent hours listening to North Meadow Creek as I sit on the old red bench over the root cellar, seen the whitetails play and the red fox jump in the pasture to the north. There are owls in the cottonwoods and cranes in the slew and bats that slurp up the night bugs. I've had one lost moose, a couple of curious bears and a single (well, he might have been married) recalcitrant badger wander through. I can look over the lake, down at the canyon and up at the mountains that touch the sky. There is something comforting in all that.

It's a grizzled and venerable shack—Tarpaper Acre—with all those wise and talking walls so common to the well lived-in shanty. It is creaky and strange, the site of 100 years of smiles and tears and God knows what else. This summer—in order to help pay the mortgage—I suppose I will rent part of it out to the fisherman and travelers who pass through these parts for their brief pleasure. Maybe they will feel just a little bit of what I feel when I plop down and wonder over the sights to which the house has borne silent witness, maybe not. I hope so, but it doesn't really matter.

I've never bought a house before, as my theory of life has consistently been one of gettin' while the gettin' is good. A home has always seemed too permanent for one that the cosmic podiatrist has diagnosed as possessing perpetually itchy feet. Still, for some reason, this is different.

A man's home is his castle, however it takes more than great halls, elaborate turrets and priceless tapestries to make a castle a home. As with people, the scars and blemishes of time, the lessons of age and experience and a life lived full, are what bring out the greatest sense of character.

This castle is mine. This castle has character.

With a little luck maybe some of it will rub off.

Nights In White Satin

*T*he satin sheets are on the mountain tonight, a fine and shining white that appeared just yesterday past and stretches wide its arms with a seductive promise of the languid days ahead. Out in the foothills of the Tobacco Root range you can see it slipping from the sky, tumbling down slowly in a sort of meteorological foreplay. Rock and snow meet and embrace in the dance of the seasons, preparing with shy smile and quiet joy for the cold months just beyond the calendar's horizon.

Some dread winter. They feel that—like the lonely guest—it arrives too soon and departs too late. They say it lasts forever, the sub-zeroes crawling between the cracks of house and mind and stealing the life from life, but on that point I disagree.

Spring is fine and fall is grand and the summer shouts with the enthusiasm of a teenager in full rut. Still, to me, winter is the best. It is quiet and peaceful, a frozen vintage with a dry wit. It is the place where I hibernate and recharge and think thoughts that time does not allow when the sun is close. It is the sharp crack of smoldering logs, the fragrant tang of just poured brandy and the camaraderie of those who make this high place—my place—their home year round.

Winter, you see, requires thought and respect. Is the wood in? Is the fuel tank full? Are there books on the shelves and ample food for the pup? Have the jumper cables, matches, gloves, boots, water jug, sleeping bag and jar of peanut butter been stowed in the back of the truck? How about socks and long johns? Did you remember the sawed-off? Are the tires worn? Can the block heater survive another year? Where's that dumb looking Arctic hat?

See? Winter makes the mind work and the body relax. It is that blissful period when one can stay close to home and realize what home really means. For those of the hermit bent the season of cryogenic slumber is especially nice, for no excuses are required for solitude. Small wonder I like it.

Long ago, when I was more young than now and much more stupid (yes, the latter is possible, believe it or not) I swore I would never live in a place where the mercury dipped below 70°. I pursued and captured that early oath, spending near a decade sweating it out on the shores of the southern Gulf, but soon realized that my hasty words were ill spoken. A non-broken eternity of sugar sand beaches, six foot blond bikinis and smoking reggae bands hold undeniable charms—and while I might desire at least one of those attractions on any given day—I need the seasons much more than I need glittering sand, flashy flesh or the steel drum backbeat of Bob Marley and the Wailers. Specifically I need one season.

That season is but a blink away.

The neighbors figured I was a little weird—and didn't mind winter—during the year before last. Buffett the wolfhound was young, yet heavily dedicated in training me to sit, heel and stay. In the dead of February we trudged the gravel road in front of Tarpaper Acre for hours at a time—temperatures some days at 20° below. Buff wore his heavy winter jacket. I was dressed in layers of makeshift gear—arms and legs stiff—looking a bit like the Michelin Man in traction. The days were quiet and serene and merely discovering we had avoided frostbite was a joy.

I never did figure how to sit, heel or stay, but that blessed return to the indoors far outweighed my learning disabilities. Buff would hit the chow, I would hit the coffee. Coffee has never tasted so good before or since. I avoided the chow and can't comment.

It's still a ways off—those winter days—but I can smell them in the air and feel them in the bones. A goodly number of folks assume winter is the dead time, simply because they are taught to associate life with the first sparkle of green shoots and the gangly sprint of young things. It is hardly dead. Winter may be sleepy, but "to sleep...perchance to dream." Without Winter—as I learned in the southland—it is hard to appreciate anything else. It makes you wonder and it makes you grateful and is beautiful for its own sake.

Winter is coming. It is near. I relish the thought of seclusion and silence in equal measure to the thought of good friends who come calling for a barbecue during a mid-February snowstorm.

I like winter. I like people who like winter, and even those who tolerate it grudgingly but tough it out nonetheless. Enduring winter with a smile (or grimace) says something about bloodlines and character—who you are and what you do.

Should you pass this way, I'll be the one smiling.

Seven Whitetails

*T*here were seven whitetail deer outside my door this evening. I suppose that, to many people, this is not a big deal. I mean, we're hardly in short supply of whitetails way up here on the third vertebra of the backbone of the world. Walk out the door or drive down the gravel road at any given time and you are like as not to spy deer or antelope or some other hill dweller who has decided that a fine and easy meal lies waiting in the wind-blown pastures.

Still, it's a big deal to me, and for that I'm thankful. The pulse of adrenaline, the electrical spark that travels my spine whenever I receive a close encounter of the critter kind, is something I would not wish to forfeit. Lose that feeling and I guess I lose everything. Frankly, I sometimes feel I've lost enough things, which is not so much a whine but rather a cryptic glimpse of my own personal nostalgia. It took a long time to find something I wanted to hold tightly—these snowy mountains, those blinding stars, the singing rivers and boldly shy whitetails—and I would not allow them to go away without a bitter and deadly fight. Maybe they are as important as life itself because, to me, they are life itself.

The sight of the whitetails, crackling energy engaged in the race of basic survival, the white hot feeling of excitement inherent to the furtive glance, the cleansing rush of a brisk mountain gale whistling 'round my heart as the tan beauties sail silently over the fifth wire, allows me to know that I've yet to take the real things for granted. It whispers, despite my deep sense the world will drive itself to hell in a hand-cart given half a chance, that there is yet joy. It cries out, despite my intrinsic belief that most folks make decisions based upon faulty reasoning and self-delusion, that the planet and its inhabitants can display majesty when least expected.

In some weird way, the presence of unbidden wildness makes me feel that love can and will prevail, at least some of the time. It sends the message that, when the audience departs and our kind ignores the critical eye of judgmental peers, we can be kind and giving. Shakespeare was right, all the world is a stage, unfortunately most of us are amateur thespians who have never learned the difference between our parts and our conscience. But, in those brief moments when we become honest humans rather than fictional characters, the world is ablaze with light.

I am, was and most likely forever will be a cynical sort of hick. I'm a believer in the proposition that while all men might be created equal, some are created a lot more equal than others. I generally feel that most of the problems of the human race derive from man's inability to keep his fat nose out of somebody else's business. This goes for individuals as well as government, and is something of a corollary to what killed the cat. It's the thing that gets me riled at politics, the thing that raises my dander when a busybody attempts to question, pry, invade or coerce without formal invite.

The hermit mentality is not really comprised of disgust with one's own species, that's just a convenient fallacy created by folks who can't be by themselves for more than two seconds. It is, to be quite honest, simply built upon the personal belief that courtesy and character surpass all other virtues. It involves knowing one's self better than one knows others. It is not a quest for wisdom so much as the search to learn and understand, to translate the torn and faded pages found in the library of soul.

So I'm glad for the visit of the whitetails. I'm glad for the unsuspected smile and silent laugh that breaks my lips upon the astonishing arrival of such welcome wraiths. They give me the wonder of surprise, and make me glad that the ability to be surprised has not totally boiled from my blood. I don't look for them, which makes their presence all the better. They, and their various kin, are as necessary to my life as spare ribs, oxygen, mountains and silence.

I am about to check another year off the calendar. As always—and as we never believed when we were children—each month goes by more quickly and each day grows shorter. I was wondering what kind of pretty I truly wanted, how I should mark such an inauspicious occasion. It strikes me that, maybe the finest present would be to always remember to see the glorious sights that surround us all, every second. The places, creatures and even people that entice me—seduce me—to hang around and see how this story ends.

The whitetails sent that gift, brightly decorated and magnificently startling.

I will thank them the next time they drop by.

A Moment In Time

*T*ime is an elusive quality, something that can't be grasped, held, hoarded or saved. It is a non-tangible entity with which humanity is obsessed. In the rush to make more money, accomplish more tasks and make a discernible mark on the world, most people find their precious hours slipping away unnoticed. We contemplate cluttered desks and too full plates, jabbing multiple irons into the fire with the frenzied enthusiasm of a demented blacksmith. We run and rush and hurry as if we are trying to cheat the calendar. In the process we not only fail to smell the roses, we dash past the entire garden with barely a notice. There's always tomorrow, we think.

It strikes me that something gets lost in the tangle of all this self-inflicted hustle and bustle. That something is ourselves.

I suppose I am noticing the encroachment of time because it is March. To me, March has always been a smirking trickster with delusions of green. It is the waiting room of months, a four week span whose arrival I anticipate with a glee that never moves quite quickly enough to suit.

In the Ozarks, March was the onset of spring, the time to hit the fishing hole despite the fact that skims of ice still dotted the water's surface and nothing would bite for at least another 30 days. It was hopeful and serene, a hint and a promise. In contrast, March in Margaritaville was no different from January, June or October. The palm trees chattered and swayed in the sub-tropical breeze. Tiny Gulf breakers sizzled at sand's edge and the beach people wandered the streets in that humidity based semi-stupor that is the natural offshoot of paradise paralysis.

The Rockies are another story entirely. March blusters and blows and covers the earth with a blinding blanket of white. Cabin fever is at its peak, and one has no idea if or when the warm days will arrive. Spring does not descend gently here on the third vertebra of the backbone of the world. It drops like a rock between the hours of 1:00—3:00 p.m. on an undetermined Saturday in June, a climatic leap twixt the chasm of winter and summer occurring in the blink of an eye.

Still, some internal body clock whispers in the darkness that the change is on its way. Unfortunately in March, in my haste for something better, I generally let this perfectly good month pass by without thought. I tend to forget that time marches on. That's either a shame or a crime or both.

Then again, perhaps it is more than just this particular season that forces me to notice the modern human tendency to pack tightly our days with frustration and trivia. Perhaps it is the ever expanding attitude that a lack of non-stop productivity is some sort of deadly sin. I once had a partner who was at a loss to understand how I could lie around for hours in a half doze, doing nothing but staring at cotton ball clouds and drinking from the well of imagination. "How can you sleep your life away," he would ask.

"You stick with your strengths, I'll stick with mine" I would sarcastically reply.

You see, I have a theory that the slow stroll, the quiet days and languid nights, are just as important as the frenetic quest for fame and glory. Such times—whether tossing a line on a mountain lake, conversing with a friend or simply stretching cat-like under a warm sun—recharge us in body, mind and soul. They give perspective. They allow us to both think and see clearly. Slowing down allows us to know life, and brings the wisdom that haste doesn't make waste, it is waste.

Today's tomorrow is yesterday. My father used to say that, and I finally understand what it means. Run too fast, try too hard, and you will miss the things that are of true value and importance. Slow the pace, inhale deeply and you will find treasures beyond reckoning. Every day I find this thought to be more true than before. Time is not of the essence. Time is the essence.

I came to the high country, in large part, out of frustration with the insistent desires of modern society down below. The mountains are great teachers, standing silent and unbending, measuring time in millennia rather than minutes. Watch them long enough and you will come to know that, more often than not, the simple things are the things that matter.

It is March, and I should not let it pass. Today I will watch the mountains and clouds.

If I'm smart, I'll do it again tomorrow.

Love & War

*L*ove, at least the stereotypical romantic version, is more exhausting than friendship. The former demands constant reassurance and continuous proof, whereas the latter is a master of the give and take approach. One can cause insult to a friend—create hurt feelings or forget an invitation—and the offense will be forgotten with a shrug of the shoulders and a tilt of the mug. Conversely, to inadvertently bruise the feelings of a lover is to incur guilt and wrath, the silent hurling of emotional trip-wires. Scratch a lover and discover an adversary. Scratch a friend and they might ask for a Band-aid.

I have never quite figured out this paradox—which isn't surprising since not a single soul in the course of human history has figured it out either—however it is still one of those ultimate truths which causes no small amount of consternation. It is one of the main reasons why I have chosen the modified hermit's road, the path of glorious solitude intertwined with chance meetings, wonderful moments and deep friendships spread across a continent. Although it took years to understand the lesson in regards to my own life—and admittedly there have been numerous, regrettable set-backs along the way—I did finally stumble across a compromise with my own soul. Ironically, that compromise taught me that nothing is more destructive than a compromise of convictions.

The lesson? To thine own self be true, no matter how much irritation it causes. Kindness to others is paramount, but of a somewhat penultimate nature. You see, altruism should not (cannot?) come at the expense of your own values and beliefs. Fine things need not last forever, they need only to be fine. One need not own the jewel to appreciate its beauty. I realized this fact only when I realized I had, at times, attempted to inflict that which I hate upon others. When love is based upon control, it becomes dangerous and ugly.

Do not misunderstand, passion and love are wonderful things, and possibly the highest achievement of the human soul. In modern society though, it has become popular to reduce such achievements to what we see on the screen or read on the page. As in many aspects of life, our actions are based upon fantasy. Too often our impressions of the emotions are based upon the antics of play actors. I have probably been more guilty than most of this crime of unreal passion—the search for drama and intensity is a powerful drug—however the prize at the end of such a quest is not real. The fantasy ends when the screen goes dark and we are left with little save half a warm Coke and a butter-filled pool of un-popped corn.

Yes, passion and love are marvelous, rating second and third behind true friendships, and I view them with neither cynicism nor fear. In fact they were two of many factors which led me to live in the solitude of the mountains with a large and unruly canine. Romantic love often strikes me as fraught with obsession and possession—the pressure to change, to be responsible for the life of another, to give up integral facets of personality for needless compromise. A more lasting romance, emotionally intense and far more true, is available in abundance.

I can love a mountain, for a mountain demands nothing save common sense. It defies control and provides continuous reassurance purely by the art of existing. I can love a dog (or many dogs) for it seeks nothing but friendship and kindness. It gives unconditionally, and if in a good home, receives the same. I can love the night sky and the morning sunrise, the cry of eagles and the gunshot crack of logs in a roaring blaze. I can love books and the music of the stars, the first snap of the line or the whirlygig sound of wings before the shotgun blast. I can love wise thoughts and good conversation, fine meals, true friends and the gentle transubstantiation of words into pictures. I love those things that ask nothing but acceptance and respect. I love those things that burn brightly, even if but for a second, the things that shine. I love the things that do not try and change another for their own gain or security. I love the things that listen and sing and see. The other things I can live without…and gladly without…

There is more passion and romance in a deep and foreboding mountain valley than in all the sonnets, tomes, celluloid creations and Harlequin imaginings ever created. That is what it's all about…not the oohs, and coos and unending cries for approval.

The movie said that love means never having to say you're sorry. That's both a lie and a fantasy. I'd phrase it another way.

Love means never having to say you're sorry for being yourself.

Bolts From The Blue

*T*here was a lightning storm last night, not as wicked and wild as the natural pyrotechnic display which scorched the sky on the night of July 4th, but a lightning storm nonetheless. I sat and watched devil arcs crash into the Madison Range, jagged streaks of white hot energy plowing furrows through the heavens and pan-frying the pines.

Ancient peoples would have taken this latter-day laser show for a sign, poison-tipped javelins from Mount Olympus which required the sacrifice of goat, cute virgin or wandering vagabond. As I own no goats, since cute virgins are mythic as unicorns (and also an oxymoron…I hear the last American one died around 1947) and because I was the only wandering vagabond within shouting distance, it seemed best to disregard the omen theory. This was merely a good night to seek shelter, I thought, a poor night to stand in the river with a fishing rod. A good night to scratch the dog's ears and revel in the silence. A poor night to labor on tomorrow's toils.

Maybe the last part is self-delusion, but it works for me. I'm a firm disciple from the school of "if it ain't broke, don't fix it." A person could dispute that concept—I'm broke and don't recall ever being fixed, while my dog is fixed and wasn't ever broke—but with the exception of that one semantic flaw the philosophy is more or less sound. It means that stuff like jobs should always take a backseat to stuff like watching storms and smelling flowers and chasing brown trout. Most times they don't, but we'd all be a lot happier if they did.

Lightning has a tendency to make me think deeply about the nature of life, which I guess isn't too surprising since its one of the things that make life possible. When bolts from the blue caress the earth they perform some kind of super nova/Bunsen burner effect on the soil, releasing vital nitrogen which plants suck up with a gusto. Electrical storms make the world safe for soybeans and wildflowers. They also make it more tolerable for we human types. The wonders of nature, both killer and saint, serve to remind that there are more important things in existence than promotions, the whims of tyrannical employers or the opinions of credit agencies and neighbors. They enlighten to the fact that we are bench-warmers in the big game, and would be well served to concentrate on important issues like puppies, mountains and friendship rather than deadlines, quotas and internecine squabbles.

To be honest, that's something I'd forgotten lately. The last helliday—the Fourth of July—had convinced me to go against my better nature and become a social animal. I worked a booth during the parade and jumped neck deep into festivities. I emerged intact, but tired and drawn and surly. It had been a while since I'd truly walked/worked a crowd, and now I remember why I spend most of my time hiding out in the cottonwoods behind the rickety gate of Tarpaper Acre.

I do like people, don't get me wrong, I just generally like them at a distance. Being a bit old fashioned in some respects—and basically reclusive in most others—I'm more into writing letters and jabbering aimlessly in print than holding people's court on the park soapbox. It is the nature of some folks to talk and consort and make merry with abandon. To them it's invigorating, the social equivalent of the afore-mentioned nitrogen hit. To me it's draining.

I don't neighbor well. My home is a tumble-down fortress of solitude, and it's rare that I open its doors to anyone save family or a few good friends. When the urge strikes for human companionship, I venture out. That's what out is for. Home is for quiet and safety—a place to enjoy lightning storms with the wolfhound—not a place to crank the juke and jump-start the disco ball.

So that's what we did last night—watched the fire from the sky and uttered oohs and ahhs with each successive blast. It was wild and powerful and beyond the control of the hand of man. I liked it. It served to remind that my petty problems are significant only to me, that in the grand scheme they matter less than a new bud on an old tree.

A good storm is required to clear the air, to create growth, to bring out the sights and sounds and smells which make all things seem new again.

A good storm is also required for perspective. The majesty of such a sight does more than light up the sky, it drives home a knowledge that is too easily ignored.

Yes, we're part of the show.

We're just not the most important part.

Greener Grass

I want to sail to the Dry Tortugas with a stuffed parrot on my shoulder and a cutlass in my hand. I want to speak Basque, build a moat and fire a fully automatic Uzi. I want to walk the ruins of Troy, raise a pack of wolfhounds, write 100 books and have at least two dates with Michelle Pfeiffer. I want to fly without wings or chains, build a solar house on a high mountain pass, have 47,563 pen pals, run for king of nothing and learn to play Layla on a Fender Stratocaster.

I want a lot of things, some of which I'll get and some of which—I admit—might never bear fruit. Of course, this is not to say I'm unhappy with what I have. Matter of fact, I'm downright ecstatic.

I think it's all a matter of knowing when to mow the greener grass and when to let the pasture run wild.

Greener grass is an interesting concept, and unless you have a solid rock wall on your property—or are partial to emerald tinted spectacles—it is a near certainty that the foliage will sooner or later appear more lush on the obverse of the fence. This adage is repeated often—too often—and maybe we place excessive importance on its meaning. Excessive skull sweat into such stuff kills the appetite and scares the fish—and the saying may have been intended merely as an observation of humanity's post pounding abilities and horticultural skills. Frankly though, it is my feeling that the maxim is close to absolute truth.

On the same token, it is also the greatest curse/blessing ever to leap from Pandora's box.

The curse lies in never being satisfied with what you have. It is a hex and maze accompanied by the inevitably high odds of losing things dear in the dream of potential largesse appearing with possible tomorrows. Ironically, the blessing also lies in never being satisfied with what you have. It is the joy of challenge, striving to seek and improve and question, to experience the thrill of the unknown, to learn and laugh and live life as a meteor rather than a molecule.

People always snicker when I go off on subjects of this nature. That's just dandy by me, for I feel that the world is so short of humor that any snicker is a good one, even—or perhaps especially—when it comes at my expense. I am quite secure on this particular philosophical limb, which is not so much a matter of egotism as reality. The knowledge of the subject is derived from the fact that, simply, I have a very fine fence and a very brown lawn. I come by it honest.

If we're painfully introspective, few of us are ever completely satisfied with our lot in life, and greener grass is in truth nothing but a metaphor for dreams. As with all dreams, the rapid eye movement comes in shades of rhapsody, nightmare, chimera and fantasy. The quest for greener grass is what allows people to leave urban squalor and move to places like Montana. It is the motivating factor inherent to innovation and creativity, something proven out by the fact that barbecued spareribs are tastier than raw ones. It is maybe the single most important ingredient that keeps man keeping on in the face of inestimable odds.

Conversely, greener grass is also the culprit that tempts men and women to leave hearth and home and run off to Omaha with near-total strangers. It is the best friend of the con man, scammer and Nike bedecked shyster lawyer in hot pursuit of the ambulance. It is the fire in the belly that causes duodenal ulcers rather than brainstorms.

Yes, greener grass is a metaphor for the dream, not to mention the metaphor for greed, envy and ulterior motive. Up until now I'd never metaphor I didn't like, but this one is tricky.

I like to think I recognize the difference between greener grass and astro-turf, an arrogance that has led to so many self-inflicted shots to the foot that I'm lucky to own toes. A person has to strike a happy medium somewhere (no…that's not an optimistic psychic) and I suppose the key lies in that old proverb carved into the stone arch over the Oracle at Delphi…"Know Thyself."

You see, I want to walk alone on the moon and gaze back down at the big blue ball. I want to memorize Shakespeare, deep-fry a swordfish and convert all liberals to the light side of the force. I want to watch a solar eclipse in Australia, pick the brain of Twain, tell the world's funniest joke and replace the Internet with smoke signals. I want to fly without wings or chains, discover what's really inside a Twinkie, have 47,563 pen pals, run for king of nothing and maybe just write one bestseller.

I advise that you tread carefully around greener grass. It can be loaded with bees and thorns and tigers.

Still, if you're honest with self and others, it's a very pretty walk.

Ring Of Fire

*I*t was a typical south Missouri summer. A summer where every breath filled the lungs with the smoky scent of creosote seeping from sweating fence posts, where squeaking fans barely stirred the soup of atmospheric magma and even the dogs were too tired to whine. It was a summer where the air lay heavy and wet, enveloping us in a soaking wool blanket of par-boiled humidity, where the sky dripped yet remained dropless, chuckling as the soybeans burned a sickly yellow and pond dams spackled with predatory crevices designed for unsuspecting ankles.

It was a typical south Missouri summer…almost. It was Independence Day, 1978, the closest I ever came to literally blowing my head off.

Youth is funny, imbued with the vim and vinegar of surmised immortality. We believe ourselves invulnerable, and my near decapitation came in the form of a homemade bomb. After all, it was the Fourth, and a 16 ounce Dixie Cup packed with gunpowder, firecrackers, bottle rockets and a couple of mutilated Buzz Bombs seemed a dandy family fireworks finale. Hell, I would have stuck a chain saw and acetylene torch in there if they would have fit. I was enduring and undying. I was a teenager.

This was our last true pyrotechnically inspired Fourth. My cousin landed a burning parachute on the roof, something we barely doused just before it ignited the homestead. He also dropped one on the barn and one in an extremely dry field. Our water bill was high that month.

The cousin's near torching of our property somewhat paled when my brother crammed 200 bottle rockets in a Mason jar and put fire to a gasoline soaked fuse. Initially impressive, a whooshing cascade of tiny ICBM's with explosive report lit the sky. Sadly, Mason jars are highly unstable when used as mortars. The whole mess tipped over, of course locking and loading directly at the 10 or so relatives slurping home-made vanilla ice cream and lemonade on the patio.

One Grandmother took a direct hit as a bottle rocket imbedded in her arm. Another did a long jump, beating Bob Beamon's Mexico City Olympic record by eight yards, and escaped impalement. My Aunt and Uncle dodged and ducked, Dad frowned, and Mom had a look on her face that could fry granite.

I didn't get it. In my mind this was merely a mishap, an experiment gone awry. Fireworks are clearly labeled that they should be used only under adult supervision, and adults were supervising as stipulated. They were just supervising a little more closely than intended.

Finally it was time. I set my bomb carefully in a dirt pile, drilled a small hole in the side, and laid down a 20 foot trail of gunpowder that would allow me time to fire up and take cover before detonation.

Unfortunately I had just started smoking, Unfortunately, I was a novice. Unfortunately the Marlboro slipped lip. It tumbled toward the deadly Dixie cup in slow motion as I threw an arm over my eyes and dived, which is why I still have 20-20 and a wolfhound rather than a white cane and German Shepherd. The 15 foot fireball nailed me, rising high in the sky in a primordial mushroom cloud. I staggered toward the house, barely recognizing my cousin's voice saying "Cool! Do it again!" I recall my Dad calmly walking forward, stating softly (so I didn't freak out) a phrase I will remember forever.

"Hey Ronnie, your hair's on fire."

I lucked out with first degree burns on the arms, third degree on the face, incinerated eyebrows and well done hair. I was off work the remainder of that summer, but would have gladly traded the blistered arms and hairless face for the usual sheetrock hauling. I also lucked out in that I'd neglected to pack and seal the bomb, a fortuitous move in that I would have otherwise lost my head in more than rhetorical sense. This comforted me, for I was too young to go out like Vic Morrow even though he was pretty cool on Combat.

It was our family's last big Fourth, which was maybe appropriate. I was still a kid then, but wouldn't be for much longer. The night provided an eternal Polaroid of youth, that innate sense the world revolved around me rather than vice versa. I like remembering that. It isn't and wasn't true, but it's still nice to remember.

I may shoot some Black Cats this Fourth. Most likely I'll smoke some ribs and sit on the old red bench watching the night sky and enjoying thoughts and memories taylor made for a star-bright Montana summer's eve. Though I still enjoy explosions, mortality seems closer and I'm more wary. Too much I still have to see. Too many friends I couldn't bear to leave. Too much discovery in a high mountain meadow. Too much joy in waking up with the birds rather than the alarm—enjoying the battle rather than cursing the drudgery.

That July 4th nearly two decades back was explosive in a variety of ways.

Frankly though, I'm getting a bigger blast out of today.

Buckets Of Rain

*T*he rain came this morning, as it has come for the last seven weeks, not in a raging torrent but more like the slow tears of a nostalgic spinster. It soaks ground, air, man and dog with a mild chill. Sodden clouds, tattered cotton sheets refusing to dry on the line, hang like billowing shrouds over the Tobacco Roots. A forgotten day and a forgotten scene comes to mind. A barefoot young boy and a flop-eared beagle standing in the back of a barn with bamboo pole and a freshly dug can of worms. "Rain rain go away, come again another day," we swear at the gray skies.

It didn't work then. It doesn't work now.

Still though, there is a certain acquiescent comfort that arrives with springtime in the Rockies. The snow squalls and showers and inevitable cold snaps teach that there is magic in the skies, magic upon which our child-like oaths and adult-like wishes have no effect. Our words fly away unheard in the breeze. Our desires sit silently, awaiting a fruition beyond mortal powers of creation.

It is days such as this that make us retreat and ponder, force us to seek solace in simplicity and silence. Two thousand miles to the south the ground is as dry as a dragon's laugh. Here, the dripping skies coerce the grass to grow with the speed of Jack's magic beans. Out front the wolfhound moans, that eerie call of the domestic wild. I sit in the back and wonder at the wonder.

It is a day to question and ask and gaze into the abyss. Weather is one aspect of life in which we must settle on something far less than perfection. Luckily, though many would disagree, the rest of existence provides greater leeway. I will settle for the weather. I have no choice and any other course of action is sheer folly. Settle on something less than my dreams and convictions? Not on your life.

I think I've been watching the news and reading the papers much too much recently, although that dangfool idiot box may just be the medium of most vast expression rather than causative contributor. Cutting through the gauzy propaganda of political squabbles, foreign wars, airline disasters and killer disease, there seems to be an undercurrent of settling in this country. I see it in the media ever day, and wonder how much is true.

Yes, people are settling for leaders who are hardly that. Tired of seeking a true champion, they instead tuck tail between legs and ambivalently accept pretenders who have crawled from the fast-talking ooze of the bargain basement bin. Yes, people are apathetically settling on acceptance of bizarre modes of behavior and rampant criminality. They do not wish to bring attention to themselves by stepping up to the plate and voicing opinions unpopular with the politically correct elite, and thus accept the repercussions of mute non-responsibility. Yes, people are settling on bad relationships simply because of loneliness, or conversely, leaving good relationships because of the work involved in keeping one whole.

Seems to me that a lot of people are desirous for the rewards found in a life of free will but not inclined to pay the admission fee. The prevalent philosophy seems to be a scenario from the dog ate my homework school of avoidance, a golden rule mangled in the Salad Shooter. Do stuff for others if it doesn't cost anything, and only then if others do stuff for you.

There's truth in that—such a scent is in the air—but it's not the total truth.

On a personal level I still see many who say what they think and do what they say and value honor, loyalty and courage above all else. Maybe I see it more in the rural life of Montana—and less through the media—because our lives are more intertwined than theirs. We don't have to agree, but we do have to live together. We have no cloak of invisible anonymity to hide behind, and I don't think we would want one. Maybe our lives are more simple, and in that simplicity comes a heightened sense of frankness, courtesy and personal code. Maybe we just know that if an ostrich sticks his head in the sand the best he'll end up with is a schnozz full of grit.

There are choices to be made in life, and one should be willing and able to accept the consequences of those choices. Accountability is everything. A person can have most anything they want, they just have to be willing to make the sacrifice and still live with themselves

The rain is falling. It crawls into the bones and lingers as it will. Settle on the weather, for it will do as it pleases and could care less about foolish human wants. Unlike self-imposed apathy, it will eventually go away without any effort on our part.

Settle on something less than your dreams and convictions?

There's no quicker way to drown the soul.

Asgard Smiles

*T*he Gods laughed late last Thursday evening, their inside joke punctuated with a bottomless drop of the mercury, whistling north wind and curtain of swirling white. In the way of all good jokes, the laughter started with a smile, built to a snicker and culminated in a deep-chested gale of gasping hilarity. It must have been a tale for the ages—the chortles, chuckles and guffaws lasting 24 hours as they did— and though I missed the punch line I did grasp the message.

From where I was sitting—eight miles back in the Tobacco Root Mountains under a lean-to shelter that could only have been designed by one as spatially disabled as self—the joke was at first invisible. An old friend was visiting from the tepid lands of south Florida, and having never before trekked the Montana trail, she was eager to temporarily trade the frantic charge of the crowded cities for the silent stalk of the deeper forest. It was a fine idea, and one that perhaps I needed more than she.

Change of pace is a good thing, and though I love the peaceful quiet of Tarpaper Acre and surrounding environs, I was due for that familiar scenery which is always new. These past few months have left me angry and frustrated at times—a state partially (mostly) my own fault. I had allowed my brain and soul to become too deeply involved with matters of the outside world, and was beginning to feel muddy and confused.

That's the danger, you know. The world outside the mountains has its conflicts and misguided passions, but they are restricted by the same bonds as vampires and the worst variety of mooching 10th cousins thrice removed. Such creatures can only affect you if you invite them in, and in my arrogance I had done just that. What I forgot was that mental vermin are loathe to leave without stern coercion or a swift kick.

We checked the weather, loaded the truck and headed to high places. It was the end of Indian Summer—a balmy 45°—an evening designed specifically for bright stars, rare steak, and potatoes browned in either butter or some substance that you can't believe is not butter. We talked and laughed, the whisper of breeze upon frosted tree complimented by the operatic masterpiece of South Willow Creek. As the stream cut through week-old snow, the crystal water a shimmering flow of molten diamonds performing a melody as old as time itself, I remembered to forget those many things I had purposely left behind some years before. We eventually fell asleep within the warm scent of swaying pines and under the bright smile of glistening constellations.

Sometime during the night, the Gods told a joke.

Morning swept down cold and frigid, an inch of new snow on the ground and a vicious storm sliding over the peaks. We broke camp as if the hounds of hell were on our heels. Two more inches of snow piled-up in the blink of an eye. We sliced the ropes and tarps of the shelter, tossed the unfolded sleeping bags in the truck, carried the camp stove up the hill. Another inch of snow covered my windshield. We gathered trash and whatnot, scraped the glass once more, dropped into low four-wheel and barely spun and slid our way out to the somewhat visible Forest Service path that had been a road 12 hours earlier.

We made eight miles in an hour, finally coming to more passable thoroughfares. I adore the Tobacco Roots, especially the particular section where we had settled, but do not adore them enough to become purposely stranded there. I like my fingers and toes. I'm quite attached to them and really prefer that they stay attached to me.

Back at the house, surrounded by more good friends who had arrived for the weekend, all was warmth. A few days later, as those dear to me returned to their respective homes, the quiet descended like a quilt. I sat and lit a smoke, considering those things I had recently neglected.

The outside world of here, vicious, kind and beautiful, had allowed me to recall that other, less savory aspects of the outside world are of little import to my life. The only things one needs are the things and people that matter. The only things a body requires are the things that make them happy. Chasing rainbows is fine, but arm-wrestling with smoke is a waste of a short life.

The dog whined for a scratch behind the ears. I scratched. When the earth-shaking matters of the folks down below come knocking, opening the door is completely optional. A person has to keep their sense of perspective, and more important, their sense of humor. I think maybe that the key to a good life revolves heavily around getting the joke. I hope to not forget that again.

The Gods tell good jokes, albeit cryptic and unfathomable. Still, one must never take them for granted.

Sometimes, you see, the joke is on you.

Different Spokes

I used to think that bicycles were the coolest thing in the world. Of course, I thought that when I was a kid.

Being able to not only pop a wheelie, but also ride it for 20 or so feet, was a true junior high status symbol. Coaster brakes were much neater than hand brakes because coaster brakes allowed you to power slide your Schwinn with a tremendous throwing of gravel and great scraping of knees. Three speeds made you feel if you were a streak of lightening on a midnight sky, winged feet of Hermes manning the pedals in a whipsaw blur as you accelerated beyond measurement and dopplered beyond vision. Spider handlebars and a banana seat and maybe one of those battery operated "Vroooom Motors" by Mattel (which would inevitably start by themselves at 3:00 a.m., waking up both parents and dogs) made for one fine life.

The best thing about bicycles was that they let a kid travel not only down the road, but also within the infinite Rand McNalley of imagination. I still miss my bicycle, the incredible rush I'd receive when speeding down the pond damn, but the feeling of loss is not for the bike itself but for my childhood.

You don't recover lost innocence and you don't replace pre-adolescent wonder. Those feelings are from an earlier place, something I now put on a special shelf along with long gone dogs, the first fish, dirt clod crusades fought from hay forts and love's initial smile.

I remember these things. I cherish them. I try and hold them close. They are just out of grasp nonetheless, a worn quilt that is snatched from my chin each time I retreat to its warmth.

Still, there are other things.

It is springtime in Montana, a spring which, for the life of me, I thought might never come. I love winter, for its cold walls and impenetrable silence provide me with the solitude I desire most of all but can rarely obtain, however this most recent version was a tad long even for a social misfit such as self. Too much of a good thing isn't good.

Then it happened. The mercury soared and, for a record two days in a row, the persistently roaring gales of McAllister became gentle as a shy maiden's caress. The mountain chickadees, regular diners at Tarpaper Acre since January, were replaced by bluebirds, blackbirds, robins and a three ring carnival of acrobatic finches. The grass grew up and green. The snow capped peaks smiled with life.

At night, Buffett the Wolfhound joins me on the old red bench over the root cellar. Neither of us say a word. We are transfixed by the roar of the creek, the occasional squawk of a sandhill crane and the inevitable footfalls of an unidentified something seeking filet of mouse under the shed.

Heck, I've even been raising the shades. Trust me that this is a Herculean move for one who enjoys dark corners.

It will not be long, I think, before the weather is fine enough to go up high, far away from the hated sounds of cars, phones, faxes and other associated curses of the life modern. I will go back to the spot I love most, string a lean-to tarp between skinny pines, and say hello to the world. I will dig the little pit and start the fire and sear the face of a slab of marbled red meat. I will pet the dog and throw rocks in the white-fast water and lay back at midnight and listen to stars. I will inhale earth perfume and, for a too brief time, abandon concern and forget unpleasantry. All will be gone but the immediate. Questions, answers, people and problems become a wisp of smoke that evaporates in cold night air.

I no longer ride a bicycle. I no longer want a bicycle. On hot summer days, generally when I drive up Highway 287 to a respite with friends in Pony, I will see lines of middle aged bikeniks and androgynous college types huffing, puffing and pedaling their brains out as they swim the asphalt river. I don't know these people, but I know I don't like them.

They don't ride Schwinns—their machines have designer labels—and the men and women alike sport wispy beards. They wear skin tight neoprene yuppie shorts and high tech plastic helmets that transform them into a praying mantis on wheels. I always assume these people subscribe religiously to NPR, don't eat beef and support many of the things I abhor.

They don't pedal for fun. They pedal for points. They seem to ride because they think it is part of the approved curriculum, as if you can understand and appreciate nature by impressing the politically correct social climbers at some upscale cappuccino bar.

Not for me. I drink Maxwell House.

I used to think that bicycles were the coolest thing in the world. Of course, I thought that when I was a kid. I miss those days of young wonder immensely. Still, there are other things.

And believe it or not, I like them even better.

Time Waits For No Man

I have four calendars and a clock on the wall of my little office. One calendar says it's April, another hails September, 1999. One claims we've entered into October, another announces the arrival of June, 1996.

The clock is more joke than reliable timepiece, numbers jumbled at the bottom and a big "Who Cares" emblazoned across the top. My parents gave it to me. They know their younger son quite well.

Make no mistake, time is a quantity I guard fiercely. However, the exact moment is not something with which I really concern myself. The Y2K controversy, that much-maligned millennium event when all the computers will supposedly go belly up and buy adult undergarments due to a misguided belief that they've just entered the 20th century and are plum elderly, does not weigh heavy on my soul. Heck, the clock on my computer has been screwed up ever since a lightning storm dropped by, and has consistently read August 28th, 1956 for over a year.

In short, if I'm to believe my aging Macintosh, time stopped over three decades ago on my Mom's 30th birthday. That's awful damn sentimental for a computer, but then again, Macs have always been more friendly than those stuffy IBM clones.

For the life of me, I have never understood the value of devices which mark the days and hours. Why do we need them? If it's warm outside, it's probably summer and you ought to go fishing. If the leaves are turning, Fall has arrived and you best be thinking about getting in wood and anti-freezing the truck. If you walk outside and your nose hairs freeze, winter is here and you would be well served to stay inside. If it's still snowing, but you don't frost off any fingers, then it's spring.

What's so tough about that?

I know. Folks say that they have to be organized, need to keep track of things, are required to keep appointments and be at work before the time clock buzzes. I still don't get it. If a body has created so many details for themselves that have to structure their days and hours with one of those Hell-spawned Personal Planners, then they've obviously got way too much on their plate and should slow down. Picking elderberries and looking at mountains is not a luxury one permits only when time allows. It's a vital hunk of existence.

Along the same lines, if you can't keep track of something in your head, it would appear that its importance is negligible. If a meeting is so pointless that you'll forget it without prompting, then why agree to it in the first place? If you've got work to do, why not just do it and quit worrying about the opinion of your wristwatch? Work till the job is complete or the lights go out. Get the job done and enjoy the big show.

The point here, we are graced with a paltry few minutes in this life. Time is our only true currency, and to allow others to waste it via whim, delusion or perceived sense of grandiose power is akin to self-embezzlement. There will always be those who wish to steal your time second by second, and the telemarketing buffoon, traveling Amway salesman, door-to-door evangelist, politician with a "crucial" message or boss with an "imperative" issue to discuss are heathens best ignored. Those uttering the phrase "this will only take a few minutes of your time"— the chronological body snatchers and tick tock termites—are easily put off through misdirection, guile or simple rudeness. Don't kill them right off, for the neighbors might talk. Either walk away quickly or use pepper spray. Such individuals usually don't want anything but your attention, and are merely trying to prove their industriousness by absconding with your precious hours.

This is not to say that one should ignore real obligations voluntarily assumed. If you make a promise, you keep it. You show up and do what must be done. Neither is it to imply that one should avoid doing favors for friends, family or even the guy on the street corner.

What is important is that you do these things because you either want or need to, out of an obligation to self. The decision should always be yours, whether based upon circumstance, necessity, desire or courtesy. No action should ever be taken, not a second of time wasted, just because you (or others) think it is "expected" of you.

The calendars in my office say it's April, or October, or September, or June, 1996. The clock says "Who Cares." The computer says I should send my Mom a 30th birthday card.

I look out the window and see my patch of red maples turning towards the shade of their name. The wind is blowing, the dogs are bouncing. The wood is stacked and there seems to be a slight chill in the air.

I think it's fall. That's good enough for me.

I think I'll enjoy it.

The Lost Soul

I lost my wallet a week or so back. Monetarily this isn't a big deal, for Hillbillies who write for a living 'cause they'd rather play with dogs than hang with humans aren't known for toting around a wad of Ben Franklins or a full deck of platinum American Excess cards. Truth be known, I hauled around so little in my dearly departed wallet that I remember the contents.

Let's see, there was $32 dollars, a driver's license, one Discover card, an ATM doohickey and an expired NRA membership. I only had the Discover for emergencies (defined as having an urgent need to buy an inflatable raft) and the sole reason I acquired the ATM doohickey was because visiting my bank entails a semblance of sociability and a 60 mile round trip.

There was a hunting/fishing license, the unused phone number of a chiropractor, and several business cards I've never looked at but stuck in there anyway since such seemed more polite than dropping them on the floor and saying "why the hell would I want that?"

Oh yeah. I also had a grocery store discount card which I grudgingly accepted after the check-out girl became overly-agitated when I initially refused her spiel of humongous savings. I took the thing rather than have to explain that, on the rare occasions when I'm in town, I buy burger at the first place off the interstate. Fidelity to grocery stores is silly, and should be based upon the decibel level of stomach growls. I prefer to expend my loyalty currency on bars, dogs or a small handful of friends. Good pups, fine drinking holes and steadfast buddies are tough to find. Places that sell Captain Crunch and Banquet Fried Chicken are a dime a thousand.

So anyway, I lost my wallet. I even know why, when and where I lost it. I was in a hurry, my parents were rolling into town, and I was low on both gasoline and charcoal. As my folks and I have a tendency to drive around and eat barbecued ribs I sped up to the closest Town Pump franchise, figuring a place which sells jerky, fruit pies, no-lead and usually includes a casino on the premises was sure to stock Match Light briquets.

I opened my wallet and—noting a distinctive lack of cash—placed it on the counter while I yanked out my checkbook. I paid and left. The wallet stayed. I stopped by the jerky/fruit pie/no lead/gambling hall the next day—and while the gal who took my number was real friendly—the billfold had done a Houdini.

Here's a lesson in life. Leaving your wallet in a casino is about as bright as thawing your T-Bones in a dog pound. There's a possibility your steaks and personal effects might sit unmolested, but then again there's a possibility that Bill Clinton once told the truth. The odds of enjoying a tasty meal or recovering folding green are probably a little better than betting on Janet Reno to place in the Miss Universe pageant, but probably a little worse than surviving a naked stroll on the face of the sun.

I'd guess my wallet went in a dumpster. I'd also guess my $32 bucks ended up in a keno machine. At least I lost my money by accident; the keno player lost it on purpose. Hopefully

So, I've been replacing all my government-mandated identification. This leads to maximum hassle, particularly from the credit card people.

"I've lost my wallet and credit card," I said.

"What's your account number," the card woman replied.

"How the heck would I know, it was on the card in the wallet I lost," I said.

"Don't you keep your statements," she asked.

"Lady, I try not not keep, make, or even listen to statements. I live in a state and once I ate mints, does that count?"

"Where do you live," she said.

"Montana," I replied.

"Ooooooooh," she said.

That's pretty much how it's all played out. I'll get a new driver's license one of these days, although that could be a problem because if I'm stopped on the way to get a license I'd get a ticket for driving without one. The license people also want I.D. to prove that I'm me. Just bring your license, they say.

The cast and blast permission slip and ATM doohickey will be no sweat, since I know the people who provide such things. I didn't need the business cards, and the grocery store discount was just a bunch of bologna

The NRA gets enough of my cash as is, and asking for a new membership card would only result in another fund-raising letter and a wall-sized portrait of Charlton Heston. That would be better than a glossy pin-up of the aforementioned Attorney General baring her scales and talons in the reptilian swimsuit competition, granted, but the thought of either Moses or Renosaurus greeting me with the new sunrise is frightening.

I could use that chiropractor's number.

Losing one's identity is a pain in the neck.

The Sleep...Perchance Not
To Go Stupid

I'm a firm believer that a person should always stick with their strengths. Are you a whiz at math? Become a physicist. Can you carry a tune? Pursue a career in music. Do you have a green thumb? Perhaps a life on the farm is your calling.

Like to mess around with young girls? Go into politics.

This concept, realizing your abilities and acknowledging your weaknesses, has been the primary tenet of my personal philosophical foundation. I'm never been particularly good with numbers, thus eliminating a future in accounting. I'm the first to admit that I'm so poor at sales that I couldn't convince a starving Somalian to buy a cheeseburger. I can't sing, paint, dance or draw. My mechanical know-how begins and ends with dumping the truck's ashtray.

Truth be known, if I sat down and took the time to ponder all the things at which I'm less than proficient, I would seriously have to consider whether or not I should seek a position as the eraser taster in the Number 2 pencil department of the local sheltered workshop.

Luckily, there are a couple of talents that I do possess. For one thing, I'm good with dogs. This aptitude doesn't pay exceedingly well, however it is highly enjoyable. I'm also incredibly evolved when it comes to striking a flame one-handed from a book of paper matches (learned this from Kojak reruns) and I've sucked on Marlboros long enough that

I can usually puff out a passable smoke ring. I have some limited dexterity when it comes to putting words on paper (people seem to like it best when I write "pay to the order of") and can stir up a dandy bloody mary. I've got a B.A. in barbecuing and a Doctorate in deep fryer. I even have a moderate reputation when it comes to fishing.

I didn't say catching fish. I said fishing. Sitting on the bank and watching the bobber is without doubt an accomplishment in which I excel. In fact, I'm so good at the gentle art of angling that I can even do it in my sleep.

Which brings me to the one field in which I exhibit total mastery. The art of the doze.

Oh, you bet. I can nod off at any time, at any place, in any position. Rip Van Winkle was an amateur. I once, and this is no lie, slept through a tornado. I once, and this is a lie, slept through the detonation of a nuclear warhead RIGHT OUTSIDE MY WINDOW. I've slept on planes, slept in cars (once or twice while driving) slept in school and, whenever possible, slept in my places of employment.

Some people chalk up my admiration of the nuances of narcolepsy to sheer laziness. Others claim it's my Hillbilly blood. How intolerant. I've suffered these denigrations of character in silence for many years, hurt and offended that those who prefer a waking state to sawing logs were not capable of celebrating diversity. Just another downtrodden minority, that's me. How many nights have I almost just about come awake and almost just about thought "why can't we all just get along."

That was before I read the article. Finally, there is corroboration to the importance of spending an inordinate amount of time in dreamy land.

According to the Reuters News Service, Professor Jim Horne, of the Sleep Research Center at Loughbrough University in London, has made an amazing discovery regarding shut-eye. As Doc Horne tells it, a lack of sleep can turn one into a blithering idiot.

"Sleep has been badly downgraded," says Horne. "Even in our leisure lives, sleep is seen as a waste of time."

Horne claims that many of his fellow Brits actually risk becoming mentally retarded due to an aversion to zonking out. He says that falling one hour short of eight hours sleep per night could temporarily zap one point off the ol' IQ. If a person keeps up the habit for a solid week, the intelligence quotient drops by 15 points. Assuming that the average human harbors an unlicensed IQ of 100, such a decrease in brain-wattage would quickly slide a body into the "borderline retard" level. Moreover, failure to take a regular ride on the 40 wink ferry can lead to a severe drop in reasoning skills and linguistic coherence.

Horne has no hard proof for his hypothesis. However, I truly believe that his theory explains the likes of Princess Diana, Prince Charles, Tony Blair, the Spice Girls, and the producers of all those confusing and plot-less English TV shows that don't even begin to seem mildly amusing unless you have indulged in illegal substances that make dirt and air and wallpaper seem like a danged laugh riot as well.

So there you go. Rejoice in your natural endowments. Counting sheep is a good and honorable profession. Hitting the sack with enthu-siasm and purpose can increase your potential for greatness. Keep in mind that he who vegetates, cogitates. Recall always that a siesta a day keeps the remedial reading teacher away.

Are you yawning yet?

Good. My job here is done.

Home Sweet Home

My lawn is a lush carpet of green, thick as a featherbed and abundantly sprinkled with those cute yellow flowers which are the bane of obsessive-compulsive urbanites who prefer the sterile appearance of fresh-mowed astro-turf over nature's paint by number. I like my dandelions, they break up the landscape and give it character. They also give the dogs something to sneeze over, which provides me with no end of pleasure. Anybody who can't get a chuckle out of a canine with dandelion fir up his snout is wholly unfit for civilized society.

The old firepit I rocked up is doing fine. Last Saturday's snow and last Sunday's rain dropped near two inches of much needed moisture onto the buds and blossoms surrounding this open-air kitchen, and I awoke one day to find the limbs of the trees alive with quaking emerald banners. The dense gooseberry bushes—once slumbering sticks and dulled thorns—create a temple of seclusion, the Great Wall of Gooseberry, so to speak.

Pink petals burst from the apple trees. The wildflowers are going psychedelic. I chinked mud into the fire-pit's winter cracks, erected a tripod and grill over the deep hole, and cooked up burgers with all the fixin's. The smoke puffed and the meat sizzled and the buns toasted. I don't think ground cow and a slice of bread has ever tasted so good, or ever will again. At least not since last fall. At least not till next time.

It is a fine world at the old firepit—old stumps for seats, a bench constructed of warped two by twelves, and a folding table salvaged from the dump. The pups leap and growl and smile wide as I plant myself in their domain, ecstatic that the warmth of late May has finally convinced me to once again mark time on their turf.

Red Dog sails to the stratosphere, defying gravity to snag the torn-up pair of blue jeans—his favorite toy—which I fling skyward. Crashing to Earth he rolls and prances, shaking the condemned Levis as if they were a 10 foot timber rattler, fire-breathing dragon or, maybe, a pair of worn-out pants. White dog grabs a stick, drops on his front legs, and snarls with mock ferocity. His eyes go wide and his grin lights up the dark. Though over 12 years old, a solid year of high-powered aerobics with the red menace has returned White Dog to prime health and he believes himself only four. He runs to the brush and buries his nose in the mud, proudly emerging with a naturally aged rawhide chewbone which I wouldn't touch but which he values more than gold or diamonds.

The boys know the world is right again. They realize full well that my cold season activity consists primarily of poking the wood stove and consulting with warm spirits at the watering hole. The renegade furballs who run my life and determine my schedule seem relieved that my soul has escaped winter kill. They were worried there for a minute. They surely were.

Next door, the creek is in high fever. Early warmth has brought torrents of snow pouring from the high country, and the frigid voice of the singing waters span the octaves. There's a deep bass rumble through the straightway, a tenor's melody around the bends. Whitewater smashes into brush and glides over polished stones with alto grace, and the flying droplets of misty ice provide a soprano peal. You want four part harmony? Toss out your Beach Boys albums and listen to the annual re-birth of a mountain creek. It ain't a contest. It ain't even close.

Did I mention? I think that spring has finally arrived.

I sit on the back porch, drink my coffee and light a cancer stick. I'm blessed with the world's largest back porch—the floor packed with worn chairs and tables, the walls covered with rusty traps, ancient wagon wheels, dented pots and a plethora of saws and grass scythes and the like. During the warm times the porch becomes my defacto living room. There's an old shack and ancient corral just a stone's throw up the steep hill behind my place, located on the ranch that borders my little chunk of heaven. The deer like it, and though I really wish my pups would quit trying to make friends with them—so do the skunks and porcupines.

The wind chimes catch a hint of breeze and play me a lost symphony. The finches are back—they're sucking down black thistle seed like it's 40 year old Scotch. I broke down and bought a smoker this year, and combined with some hickory wood I snatched from a friend's place in Missouri, rib nirvana is always but an hour or so away.

It's just an ordinary day in this extraordinary place where I live. Not much hustle and hardly any bustle. There's such a perfect beauty in the slow grandeur of this best of seasons, such a tranquil wisdom, that time seems to fly. I love spring's arrival. I dread its passage.

But for a little while, it's all mine.

Charge Of The Dog Brigade

*T*he charge of the dog brigade begins each morning at approximately 7:00 a.m. First comes a rustle of movement from the far end of house, the anxious troops shifting in place, gathering strength and finalizing strategy. Next comes a thundering of paws, a barely muffled kamikaze dash across worn carpet followed by the sliding click of claws upon kitchen tile.

Last comes the assault. Red Dog leaps high, landing smack on the stomach of the gray-bearded human who has come to expect the onslaught. White Dog rears on his back legs—a cross between Trigger the Wonder Horse and a ticked-off grizzly,—batting the air, grinning huge and occasionally taking an inadvertent swipe of flesh from the aforementioned aging human's right arm.

Finally, after five minutes of mock growls, scratched ears, face licks and no small amount of grumbling (the latter emanating solely from your's truly) I stagger from the bedroom and throw wide the doors. Nearly knocked over by their second charge, I dodge and stumble and grab at walls as the Dog Brigade races toward the great outside. Intent on the successful completion of their next mission—defined as barking insanely while patrolling the perimeter for uninvited cats, skunks, porcupines or mule deer—they are blissfully unaware of any trials and tribulations which the world might offer.

They know only joy, the ecstasy of fresh-baked sunrise and the heady draught of chill air sliding down off the big mountain. They see only the promise of unimaginable adventure, the ripping asunder of old shoes or the addictive roll in a patch of muddy snow. They hear only the wind in the trees, the silent rustle of field mice diving for cover, and perhaps the purity of their own thoughts.

Ahhhh...to be a dog. Although I normally find routine to be a pox upon sanity, this daily regimen is one I treasure, worth far more than gold, diamonds or the tidbits of success so vital to those who strive endlessly for the flimsy status of an obese checking account. Without it, life would be gray and dark. Without it, though I would no doubt still arise from slumber and trudge through the day, existence would seem bland as broth.

I suppose I spend too much time with the canines, or so say some of the old friends who live in the overly-populated asylums down below. They tell me I should become more involved with my own kind, that I should travel widely, fraternize freely and focus my energies upon acquisition. That I should become a member of "normal" society.

Hogwash. I don't need many things, I say, for I have the dogs. I venture out when the urge strikes, I say, for I live in a fine little outpost where, should they so choose, the hairy ones are welcome to tag along and share conversation. I am uncomfortable with travel, I say, for though the dogs enjoy rides in the truck, they become bored after an hour. As for society, I find it highly unsociable. The barks of bipeds often involve perfidious intent. The fur and fang set, however, demonstrate unwavering fidelity both in word and deed.

I've been forgetting this wisdom of late—these good lessons imparted by the dogs—much to my own detriment. One must earn a living, and recent requirements of my peculiar profession have sometimes left me surly as a wino at the annual Baptist picnic. Voluntary obligations these are, things needed to secure the life I've chosen, and thus there is no regret. The unpleasant aspects of the tasks (little more than leaving home for short spells and speaking with strangers) will last but a brief time. Still, a deviation from one's adopted philosophy tends to muddy the mind's waters.

I was in such a discombobulated state last evening, and thus reached for a much-loved book. Although I rarely read Chinese philosophy these days (opting instead for Stephen King or The Old Farmer's Almanac) I unearthed a comforting pearl of wisdom in the ancient writings of Lao Tzu.

"Heaviness is the root of lightness. Serenity is the master of restlessness," wrote the venerable one. "Therefore, the Sage, traveling all day, does not part with the baggage wagon. Though there may be gorgeous sights to see, he stays at ease in his own home."

The translation? One need not go into the world to appreciate the world. One need not be constantly surrounded by people to enjoy the reality of their friendship. One need not strive to achieve great fortune, for wealth of the soul is diminished by pursuit of the transient. Honest contentment lies not in searching for amazement, but rather in noticing the miraculous wonders inherent to the obvious and simple.

It's that ol' home, sweet home deal. The realization that, while one could rush about the planet in a vain attempt to smell all the roses, those pretty flowers will never have a scent as sweet as those found in your own back yard.

The dogs know this.

And, though they must remind me on a daily basis, I do too.

May You Fare Well

Death is a funny thing, especially the deaths of those whom we love. Although we believe the world should come to a grinding halt in respect for our sadness, should share in our tragedy with weeks of silence, the world has a tendency to be uncooperative. The phones still ring and the mail still arrives and the Rocky Mountain spring vacillates between sun and snow and winds that blow.

By the time this column sees print, one of my best friends will have been gone for several weeks. Within such a brief span of time, I am quite certain, the life and death of David T. Hays—mountain hermit, lover of critters and my defacto partner in a wide array of literary terrorist antics and odd publishing endeavors—will have been examined microbe by microbe and analyzed into the ground. Those who knew him well will still grieve. However, through a veil of tears and a fog of fractious dreams we will keep in mind that the death of a man is far less important than the way he lived.

David Hays lived well. He lived odd, but he lived well.

I suppose I knew David better than most and less than some. I could be wrong in this—and numerous folks will undoubtedly swear that I am—but I'm not sure anyone ever really knew him completely. His life, by choice, was one of intense solitude intermixed with a not infinitesimal amount of fame and deep emotion. David played his cards close to the chest, and allowed different folks to know different tidbits of information regarding his past and present dependent solely upon his mood at the time. Perhaps that's something we all do. It just seemed that David kept his secrets and shared his thoughts on a larger scale.

Defining David is not an easy task, for the life he led after coming to Island Park, Idaho in the early 1980's is filled with (mostly) pleasant contradictions. He honestly loved the birds, animals, trees and creeks that surrounded, and sometimes shared, his plumbing-impaired, 14 x 14 Idaho shack. He cherished and demanded his privacy. On the other hand, he was a prolific writer—and a damned fine one at that—who seemed to enjoy good conversation and correspondence with folks all over the country. He wrote often of his philosophy and was published widely. Still he detested those days when overly-obsessed readers would track him down and badger him to become their mentor.

"I ain't no Guru," he once laughingly told me, relating the story of some cretin who was pestering him incessantly. "Not unless they pay a lot of cash."

I don't think David would have hurt a fly, unless of course the fly walked upright, got in his face and attempted to play supplicant at the well of wisdom. He hated that stuff. Some of the messages most common to his writings were the need for independent thought, self reliance and rugged individualism. I think he felt that those who couldn't pick their own apples from the tree of knowledge were missing the point, that they either hadn't read, hadn't listened or hadn't grown up. Whichever the case, I know they were a pain in his neck.

Fact of the matter; there were two versions of David Hays. At least. There was the man, and then there was the myth. I never really knew about the myth until after I knew the man, and in that case I consider myself fortunate.

I would venture a guess that most folks knew Dave from his written words, saw only his reverence for nature and the joy of simple life he so beautifully illustrated through his newspaper, columns and book. I would surmise that most knew him as the legitimate romantic he was, read his portrayal of his life and loves and envied the depth of emotion.

I would believe that most folks saw him only as the wandering minstrel who had adopted the ways of the east—actually went there and studied them, none of this New Age mail order nonsense—with a deadly serious demeanor.

These are good things. These are true things. These were aspects of the personality.

But there was a lot more, and most of it was just plain fun.

I met David Hays when sent to interview him for a feature story. I didn't know the guy from Adam, and considered the job just another writing task. David didn't know me either, but the intended 30 minute interview turned into three hours of good talk, good laughs and the beginning of a long friendship. Knowing I was unhappy in my job, he made the offhand suggestion that maybe I should start a weekly newspaper, offering any and all help he could muster.

Unbeknownst to David, I thought this was a great idea for somebody like myself, a fellow wanderer with few roots, fewer ties and a profound lack of ethical values regarding modern journalism. I immediately resigned my job, moved to Montana and started throwing the dice. I found out some years later I surprised the hell out of him when I called up out of the blue and said, "Ok, it's ready to go. You ready to help?"

He was. He did. Some of my fondest memories of David are when, in the wee hours of a Sunday morning, we would work on his Bugle and my Trout Wrapper in his ramshackle office in Island Park. Generally the place was flooded and we were in boots, computer cords tied up with twine, hanging off the floor so as to prevent inadvertent electrocution. We would scarf doughnuts, drink coffee, smoke like fiends, yak incessantly and somehow, miraculously, bash out newspapers. It used to crack us up when a passerby would walk in, see five different ashtrays puffing with six forgotten Marlboros, observe half-eaten Bear Claws and cold Maxwell House, and get a very confused look as they listened to Dave and I have a conversation on four different topics at once. Usually, they just shook their head and left.

"They don't get it," said David. He was right. People thought we should be serious with our ventures. Heck, we just wanted to have a good time, pay the bills and, if possible, write some stuff that might make a person feel or think or laugh. I'm pretty certain we did all of that. If not, I'm totally certain we had a great time trying.

The years are short and time stands still for no man. David and I helped each other out in times of broken hearts and divorce and those less than savory days when fate would throw curve balls. We would cuss and complain and finally David would laugh and say "the Gods are amused by us." We silently agreed to disagree on many issues—I think he had a heart of gold whereas I have the heart of a cynic—but we both knew that the other was as close as the phone for both good times and bad. We came to call each other brother, and we meant it. We still do. He lived and died with honor and without pity. Maybe that's all any of us can ask for.

Fly straight, David Thomas Hays. As a man you were bigger than your myth, and trust me that such is no small feat. I will think of you often and thank the stars that we met. I only hope that, wherever you are, you have discovered a place as good as that you left behind, one of those joints where the cats live forever and the eagles soar low. I see you in a land where the elk invite you out for a midnight run and the mice stay out of your sleeping bag. I envision you high on the mountain, safe within four good walls, happy with a dog-eared book and ecstatic with the woman of your dreams. I pray that the goofy smile never leaves your face, that your woodpile is full daily and that, maybe, just maybe, you've finally broken down and acquired indoor plumbing.

I'll see ya later, Big Brother. It was a good ride we took. Just the right amount of thrills and chills, twists and turns.

I just wish it could have been longer.

Back Porch Blues

*S*ome say it is the wheel, while others say it is fire. Some say it is the automobile, while others say it is the telephone, Some say it is space flight, while others say it is the personal computer. People are always debating the greatest achievement of man, searching for conclusive evidence that will, supposedly, place us a rung or two higher on the ladder of evolution than the other creatures strutting the hills and fields of planet earth.

Personally I have my doubts about man's long-term position in the evolutionary mural. To me, the human species falls far behind dogs in measurable substantive development, and is probably ranked more in the realm of goats, sheep or mules. We do have those opposable thumbs which allow us to build things—and we do possess a certain cognitive function that allows us to come up with novel ways to kill each other—but I hardly feel such minutiae assures man's future.

I can only think of one contrivance which provides a glimmer of hope that our species might actually survive and prosper throughout the misty realm of coming millennia. No, it's not atomic power, fast food or even the Marlin 45-70 Guide Gun. No, it's not Playboy magazine.

I would be referring to the creation and usage of the back porch.

Porches are, or should be, mandatory to every home in America. They are a place to sit, sleep and cogitate. They are a place to relax with your coffee, Coke, iced tea or whiskey. They are the places where problems are solved, ribs are cooked and ice cream is cranked. They are the site of quiet reflection and the locale where grief can be healed. They are a bridge between the hectic minefields of a self-serving and illogical world and the peaceful murmur of the babbling brook. They are a mental and emotional decompression chamber which prevents the chaos of modern times from giving us the intellectual and spiritual bends.

I swear, if everybody in America had a back porch on which to escape the screeching of the tube, ringing of the phone and beeping of the computer, there would soon be a mass escalation in our collective common sense quotient. We would stage a nationwide uprising and boot about 80 percent of our politicians from office. We would repeal stupid laws. We would dispense with political correctness. We would celebrate the intelligent, honor the heroic and ridicule the ridiculous. We would eat like pigs (or is that smoke a lot of pigs) laugh frequently and get real good at picking off gophers with our .22's from the easy comfort of the well-worn back porch couch. We would talk, smile, cry and think about the things which are worth talking, smiling, crying and thinking about.

Lets put it this way. If everybody in America had a back porch upon which to stay in touch with that which truly effects their lives, they'd have been a lot more concerned with Cousin Earl's sinus condition than they were with the death of a jet-setting princess. Once removed from media hypnosis, people soon realize things close to home are important, with the rest being garbage best disposed of quickly and everafter ignored.

Unfortunately, back porches aren't as common as they used to be, which strikes me as an inescapable portent of the decline and fall of man.

I'm lucky to have a world class porch, the construction of which I consider nothing short of a stroke of genius on the part of the previous owner. It's about 12 feet deep and about 40 feet long, bordering right smack against the fence line of a 10,000 acre ranch loaded with all manner of amusing critters. It looks out at trees and flowers and hills and cows. It's covered and it's cool and it catches the night breeze just enough to make my wind chimes sing.

My back porch is also loaded with, for lack of a better word, a lot of crap. However, it's good crap. We're talking wooden gates, doors, benches, and feed troughs which I salvaged from the long abandoned root cellar at my former home. There's a huge table that, apparently, once served proudly in a courtroom. There are rusty traps on the walls, along with iron wagon wheels from my late Grandmother's farm. There are pulleys and ropes and chairs and buckets and, for those times when I've had to deal with uncivilized cretins down below and the relaxation factor needs to be accelerated, a day bed.

I love my porch, as do the dogs. It keeps me sane and that keeps them happy. It is a place of contentment and fun where we keep both ourselves and each other well amused.

The back porch is the most noble invention in the history of mankind, far more important than wheel, phone, TV or computer. The only other brainstorm which even approaches the porch in magnitude of importance would be books.

And, these days, people don't use them much either.

Rules Of The Game

*T*hose who know me very well will attest all too eagerly that I have numerous inviolable rules in my life. These voluntarily imposed precepts—or commandments, dependent upon my mood—have not been inspired by any great love of organization, order or structure. In fact, nothing could be further from the truth.

I detest symmetry. That's a place where they bury dead folk. I despise categorization by degree or station unless we're talkin' weather or gas. I rebel at the very concept of the managed coterie or the finely oiled fraternal machine, with the exception, of course, of those instances where a united confederacy works in my favor without getting in my face.

A contradiction of terms or inconsistency of philosophy? No way, Bubba. An uncompromising smart alec I may sometimes be, but then again, I never claimed to be a team player. I'm a selfish, stubborn and often egomaniacal bearded hillbilly, and I'll be the first to proudly admit it. That's one of the reasons I live in a far-back place and associate only with my pups and a few close relatives and confidants. Hell, most of the time I won't even answer the phone. The doormat says "Go Away."

Here's why.

Our days are simply too fleeting to waste them on the uninvited "guest" who wants to either save a soul, pick a pocket or both. Our hours are too fragile to fritter them away in fake politeness with the disembodied phone chick who wants to steal "just a moment of your time" in the hopes of winning you over to the new and improved friends, family and hardcore-felon calling circle.

You see, my rules apply primarily to me, just as yours should apply to you. They are an anchor of sanity in an often insane world. I don't insist that others accept my rules, although one would inevitably trip across them if they were around me for very long, but neither do I gratuitously accept the rules of others. To do so would be an offense against time in a life where time is a limited commodity.

And you know what? Contrary to what modern society would have you believe, there's not a damned thing wrong with that manner of thought. It's pretty much how people lived before the creation of our paternalistic nanny state. Owning a personal code of conduct does not preclude being nice to others or extending a helping hand or listening to good advice. It simply means that you do these things when you feel like it, not when you are told you should or must.

In short, it's learning the difference between duty to self and what others expect of you.

I know. I know. In the waning decades of the 20th Century we have all been inundated with touchy-feely messages, some subtle but most not, which categorically state that we are supposed to go along to get along. We're not supposed to disagree strongly, express unpopular sentiments, or make waves that might send an unsavory ripple shimmering toward the delicate feelings of those sensitive lil' urchins splashing around the shallow end of the gene pool. We're supposed to celebrate diversity, become a part of the family of man, dive joyously into the insentient world of the single-celled organism while we stand on the side of the hill and teach the world to sing, all the time sipping Coke (diet decaffeinated, of course) and giving equality and respect to every muddle-headed nutcase in creation, even when said muddle-headed nutcases are unequal and disrespectful. To appear "appropriate" we are expected to proselytize the idiocy that "it takes a village," even when the dubious wisdom erupts from the selectively incognizant, two-faced pie hole of the queen mother of village idiots.

What nonsense. To quote Robert Heinlein, "the human race divides into those who want people to be controlled and those who have no such desire. The former are idealists acting from the highest motives for the greatest good for the greatest number. The latter are surly curmudgeons, suspicious and lacking in altruism. But, they are more comfortable neighbors than the other sort."

I couldn't agree more, and that's why I have a personal set of rules, a number of which are designed specifically to keep the former at many arms length.

What are these sacred mandates of mine? Here's a few. They're quite simple really, in a complex and confusing, totally arbitrary sort of way.

Don't leave silverware on the floor and always close the bathroom door. Let dogs do pretty much what they want, for they are smarter than us and at the top of the social and evolutionary food chain.

Fish whenever possible, and always deep-fry your catch. Buy lots of guns. Vote early and vote often. Clean out the truck at least twice a year, preferably not on the same month you bathe.

If you must speak to strangers, be strangely polite. Accept free drinks. Buy some back when the wallet allows. Barbecue at every opportunity. If a person offers kindness, be kind in turn. If they offer arrogance, betrayal, conceit, condescension or even the mildest hint of rudeness or Machiavellian intent, either walk away smiling or make them pay in a horribly painful yet creative manner. Make the punishment fit the crime. Brook no foolishness save foolishness you enjoy, and always strive to amuse yourself. This is very important, for nobody else will do it for you.

Relax. Having fun is one of the most important (maybe THE most important) aspects of life. Read a book. Watch a deer. Pet the pups. Turn on the tube. Sleep. Make sure your play time is, at the very least, equal to your work time.

Carry a concealed weapon. Carry two. Check the mirror occasionally to make certain you don't have Pop-Tart crumbs in your beard.

Make sacrifices as your conscience dictates, not the conscience (or lack thereof) of someone else. And, if you do make a sacrifice, keep quiet about it. There is a particularly warm corner of hell reserved for those who do good deeds only to make brownie points with the country club crowd. If your primary goal in life is to impress the neighbors, buy a Ferrari. Those afflicted with hard times neither require nor desire the false humanity or cloying pity of plastic Samaritans and social-climbing, armchair liberals.

Don't tell a lie unless you're dealing with a liar. Don't make a joke at another's expense unless they deserve it and/or it's a real knee-slapper. Expect nothing, for then you will be surprised by everything. Make no promises you can't keep. Hold the door for old ladies. Amuse the easily amused. Irritate the easily irritated. Don't hold a grudge unless you're sure you have the strength to carry it for the long haul. Those suckers get heavy.

Never drink whiskey under a full moon.

Cherish and trust your loved ones, and if you must make enemies, try and keep the numbers to a minimum. A body can get a powerful crick in the neck looking over their shoulder all the time. Say what you mean and mean what you say. Attempt moderation in all things, especially moderation. Always wear a shirt at the dinner table.

And that's enough of that.

Does a custom-built code of conduct lead to a lonely existence? Got me. I guess it depends upon your definition of loneliness. Personally, I've always found that living by your own rules makes for a fine life, bringing you into contact with folks who are like-minded in their quest for individuality and freedom. You might disagree with such people often and fervently—that is what happens when you encounter humans who hold title on a fully functional brain—but that very quality is what makes you enjoy their company all the more. People aren't about issues.

They are about character. Issues don't matter. Character does. Very elementary stuff.

On the other hand, perhaps the most important rule to keep in the forefront of the mind is that rules are made to be broken.

Hmmm...I don't think it's a full moon tonight.

When You Care Enough to Send The Very Least

I really don't think I'm going to send out Christmas cards this year, at least not more than the very few which will be received by family and close friends who truly deserve them. The tradition of blanketing the faded names in my address book with mass produced holiday cheer has always sort of bothered me. I'm actually ashamed of myself that I ever got in the habit of proffering such psuedo-sentiments at all,

For half a decade or so I sat around with my list during the first week in December and addressed a hundred or more reindeer emblazoned greetings to folks with whom I'd totally or almost lost touch, folks who would in turn send me the same type of negative exertion, annual missive. I would send them to business associates with whom I had never spoken socially, friends with whom I hadn't spoken for over a decade, and acquaintances to whom I occasionally spoke but didn't really say anything.

The effort did and does strike me as somehow pointless and false and disgustingly effusive. The advertising campaigns of the Christmas card biz may attempt to tell me that I'm a fine person because "I care enough to send the very best," but such is nothing but a line invented to help the non-communicative ease a guilty conscience. If I really cared enough to send the very best I would sit down in June or February or October and write the long departed comrades a deep and heart-felt letter. I would make a phone call, or perhaps even hop on a plane for a visit. I could do many things, but scratching my John Hancock on a cheap card containing little save a signature and a computer printed holiday rhyme invented by some cubicle geek in the Hallmark home office wouldn't be one of them.

People often send cards not because they want to, but rather (as is also true with most Christmas gifts) because they have been convinced by retailers and the media that such is their obligation. That, my friends, is the worst kind of Yuletide hogwash, and the spinmeisters who promulgate such guilt on a susceptible public are undoubtedly bound for a particularly hot section of Hades.

Such being the case, I am here and now boycotting the entire process.

Some people decide to personalize their Christmas cards with a form letter. Although I've read a couple of these things that I thought were pretty amusing (printing such a letter on stationary from the local penitentiary is a good start) for the most part they provide a ton of information that most of the recipients don't understand because they communicate with the senders once a year and then only via Christmas cards. The form letters generally impart info such as "Johnny hardly ever wets the bed these days and Mary Jo's teacher tells us that she is the best finger painter she has ever seen in 46 years of remedial education."

Frankly, upon digesting such revelations, I generally sit down, scratch my head and go "Huh…I didn't know that those guys had kids."

Some members of the mandatory Christmas card exchange like to have a family portrait taken, something they can spam across America in order that their long lost chums can cherish their appearance in the here and now. This can be depressing. Maybe it's just me, but if I haven't seen or personally spoken to someone in a couple of decades I assume that they are relegated to the personal nostalgia aisle, that they are a part of my past that should stay in the cozy corner where I've tucked it. I'd prefer to remember them as they were—allowing the gift of memory's eternal youth—rather than witness photographic evidence of pot guts, gleaming pates, missing limbs and a brood of drooling, acne covered urchins who are lifting the dog by his tail.

Now don't get me wrong. If these same people showed up out of the blue at my Pony, Montana rib shack I would welcome them gladly and provide at least a half rack and all the Budweiser they could swallow. That would be because they did something neat that entailed effort and displayed true fellowship. However, since Christmas cards require no effort, I'd just as soon that folks who are no longer in my life keep their guts, bald heads and poodle swinging zit factories to themselves. I enjoy thinking of them as hippies on motorcycles, witty rednecks or gorgeous beach babes. I don't want to know about their prostate surgery, liposuction, fourth kid or sixth divorce. It dates me.

I believe my new Christmas tradition will be to share Christmas with those who are an active and vital part of my life, which is how it always should have been in the first place. I believe I will make a better effort to keep in touch with my loved ones during the year, and let them know that we're still a part of each other's lives.

I don't need or want Christmas card acquaintances.

But I'll take all the real friends I can get.

The Squeaking Nostalgias

*I*t is a Monday, three days before Thanksgiving. I really should be cleaning the house—especially since White Dog has experienced some intestinal distress of late and the old homestead possesses a rather pungent fragrance. I strongly believe holiday guests should not be subjected to unsightly carpets and odd odors, and while I'm sure the task will be completed before their arrival, today I'm just not in the mood.

It's one of those days where I've been thinking too much, and thus have attempted to keep myself busy with chores of a more physical nature—running the chain saw, splitting several weeks worth of wood, cleaning the garage and any other task which temporarily muzzles the mental dialogue. There is usually an oblivious solace in sweat work—though I know to utter such a thought is an affront to my Hillbilly reputation—and on this cold November afternoon mental oblivion seems a rather cozy locale.

Cozy, but apparently unobtainable, as I'm now writing a rather maudlin column.

You see, I've got a bad case of the squeaking nostalgias.

The highly illustrated tapestries of things long gone have a tendency to creep up on everyone from time to time, but I think they may hit a tad more severe in the case of those who were fated to tread solitary paths, those that were born on the hermit's highway. You remember a very special Christmas tree—one saved from the dumpster—surrounded by small packages, the air resplendent with the smell of cinnamon steam arising from the woodstove's teapot. You recall special nights in front of a blazing fire pit, blue checkered cloth thrown over a ramshackle aluminum table and covered with the summer's first picnic. You catch a glimpse of smiles, the far distant sound of laughter, huge Chinese feasts and the memory of terrible movies.

You remember friends, dogs and relatives that have come and gone—some dead, some living, a few somewhere in between—and though for a moment there is a twinge of the old happiness, such memories are soon replaced by the knowledge that what once was is no longer, and will never be again. Chasing your past is little but a delusional treadmill.

Ok, this is sounding too glum and philosophical even for me, and trust that such is no small feat. I suppose I'm just one of those people who get a little strange (make that "stranger") around the holidays. I get to thinking about the world as it is and the world as I'd like it to be, ruminating on successes, mistakes and all sorts of dumb esoterica which would be better off shoved into the brain's back closet till it's coated with a thick layer of protective dust.

No such luck on this day. Somebody has done went and gone goofy with a large, economy-sized can of metaphysical Endust. Construction of this particular wall won't start till later. One more brick in a collection of mawkish masonry, a barrier capable of being scaled only by all hounds, trusted friends and dear family.

Truth be known, I am hit this afternoon with the ridiculous desire to analyze the human race, wondering if the outward appearance of our species is frequently diametrically opposed to the truth. Those that show little emotion often do so not because they're unfeeling, but rather because they feel too much. Those who display emotion like a spill of spring rain are often hiding old hurts, trying to grasp something which they always sought but never captured. We wear many masks, and though I've said it before, the hardest jobs in the world consist of being yourself, knowing what you want, and making tough decisions full in the knowledge that you may regret them a month, a year or a lifetime down the road.

I suppose stuff changes; such is the nature of the beast. Many like to say that change is good, but it strikes me that change can just as easily be hideous. I guess one of the most perplexing aspects of change lies in how humans wish to change one another, how the qualities that drew them together in the first place become the things they wish to eliminate. A weird tribe, we are.

However, here's a little secret. You can change people. You just can't do it for very long. Moreover, the result will always be loss for all involved. It's a lot like that teakettle on the stove. You can heat the water. You can even watch it boil. Unfortunately, that churning substance soon disappears, evaporated into thin air until such time as it returns to its original form in another place.

I doubt the world will ever learn this, but I'll say it anyway. Ron's little lesson for the day, and a cliché lesson at that. It is far worse to have something and not want it than to want something and not have it.

And with that, we walked our separate ways. No malice, no anger, no harsh words. Just some lingering condensation on the kettle and a hint of transient sadness.

And, perhaps, one last wisp of steam which vanished in the gray November sky.

Spring Snow

*I*t began to snow last evening, a fine mist of powdery white which lost its footing on the ragged bowl of the big hollow mountain and slid softly into the back yard of Hermit's Heaven. The pups ran and barked, red dog rolling and tumbling while white dog buried his nose and inhaled the sweet nectar of winter's scent. Though they invited me to join them, I declined the boys' gracious offer. I bark too much as it is, and believe running was designed primarily for moonshiners, chicken thieves and Yankees. Moreover, sticking my snout into the drifts would necessitate firing up another Marlboro.

Such being the case, I simply grabbed a few more logs, opened wide the damper, and enjoyed the midnight performance of the canine ballet. Spring storms are not normally considered a phenomenon during a Montana March, and while I'm uncertain if a little shower of flakes deserves the lofty title of honest to God storm, it's just about the closest we've come during this winter that wasn't. By all rights the squalls and blizzards should have begun last October and remained till at least May, but by my count, this is only the third or fourth time we've received even a good dusting, let alone any decent accumulation. We've had none of those dead-silent nights where the heavens are filled with glistening crystals the size of silver dollars and pie plates. We've had none of the bone-cracking cold that sends you to the warm refuge of old quilts and smelly critters. We've had only a sparse few days where you could really tell it was winter at all.

Some people think I'm nuts for my addiction to atmosphere ala mode. They count their lucky stars for those temperate times when it isn't necessary to scrape the windshield, plug in the block heater, don the long handles or continuously feed both stove and wood box. All I can say is that a monotone climate—no matter how mild or pleasant—sucks quite a bit of the anticipation and wonder from life. I like my seasons very well defined, thank you very much. A drastic and noticeable change in the meteorological milieu means that I don't have to consult the calendar. When it snows, it's winter. When it doesn't snow, it's (normally) not. Moderation is for monks, and a moderate interval like we've experienced over the last few months screws me up to no end.

What is it anyway? June? November?

I suppose that part of the reason for my amicable relationship with semi-glacial conditions revolves around the fact that I write for a living and thus rarely have to leave the property (sliding down to the bar and smoking a few dozen racks of ribs doesn't count). It's not like I ski or run a snow machine or build igloos or something. I don't have a dog team in the traditional sense (my guys think that "mush" is what you lick out of the bottom of the wastebasket). I don't run a trapline, and I quit ice fishing a couple years back out of sheer laziness.

Winter activity is not my specialty. Winter inactivity…now that's another story.

I like winter because it is slow and easy and quiet, a time when the sun arrives fashionably late and departs at a well-mannered and respectable hour. It is a time for good sleep (something at which Hillbillies are highly qualified) good meals, blazing infernos, hot cider and mental detachment. To me, there is a blissful isolation about winter that sings of contentment and peace and safety. It's that one happy time where even the Seven Deadly Sins take a break, offering a special dispensation for those wishing to perfect the art of creative sloth.

There is a rumor floating around that this present bout of the flurries may last for several days, may actually pile up to such a degree that there is a satisfying crunch underfoot. Perhaps the sky has finally gone off strike, is ready to go back to work after it's long period of indolent ambition. A foot would be nice. Two would be better. Three feet might even lead me into forgiving what has up till now been a rather lack-adaisical attitude on the part of the Jack Frost contingent. But, I'll take what I can get.

White dog and red dog wish to go outside....again. Their coats are finally dry, the packed ice has melted from their paws, they've had a brief nap. They run out the door and bark, rolling and tumbling and inhaling the sweet nectar of winter's scent.

I grab another log and feel the pulsating heat of the stove. I don't tell them that winter will soon be gone, that such things are fleeting, that they should enjoy it while they can.

You see, unlike me, they know better. They enjoy it not for what it could be, and not for what it should be.

They enjoy it for what it is.

Two Score Years

I was born in November of 1959, on the 13th day of the month. It was a Friday. That was the same night Glenn's Cafe blew up, a gas explosion that sent a fiery mushroom cloud into the black Missouri sky. The joint went boom at the exact second Mom and Dad drove past it on the way to the delivery room of our county's sole rural hospital. Dad dropped Mom at the entrance and, being on the fire department, both sent out the alarm and spent the rest of the night preventing the town from becoming a giant space heater.

I've written about this before, and thus won't go into details again. Suffice it to say that, as a believer in the power of statistical coincidence, I find the juxtaposition of these events neither surprising nor propitious. Stuff just happens, although I do wonder if a few superstitious doctors and nurses spent the early morning hours of November 13th, 1959 checking my soft little skull for a trio of tiny sixes.

By the time you read this column in one of the various publications in which it appears, I will be zeroing in on my 40th birthday. That's two score years, 480 months, or approximately 349,440 hours. It's really not a very long time, which is maybe one of the reasons it seems to have gone by so fast.

Some folks get goofy around their 40th birthday, but I don't think I'm becoming any more addled than usual. It is something of a milestone—I suppose—but not that big of one. It's more of a mile-pebble, if you ask me. I don't feel any older or more mature than I did last week, last year or even in 1990. I don't feel any urge to make major changes in my life or question my own mortality. I don't suddenly want to settle down, calm down, slow down or sit down. I might want to lay down, but, being a Hillbilly, I did and do hit the couch at every opportunity. That ain't nothin' new.

I did buy myself a giant barbecue pit for my 40th—the infamous Pony Bar-B-Q I keep babbling about—but I bought some sub shops when I was barely 20 and started a newspaper shortly after 30. These things aren't barometers of age either. If they're indicative of anything it's simply that I don't work and play well with others, and am therefore required to create some sort of phony baloney job every decade or so. This practice is kind of fun in terms of promoting mental alertness, and, after the always hectic breaking-in period, generally leaves ample time for fishing, playing with pups and the aforementioned laying on the couch.

Anyway, I took to wondering if I could honestly say I'd learned anything worthwhile in 40 years. After several weeks of thought, I actually came up with a few core beliefs. Of course, these truths apply only to me. Everybody else must find their own.

For instance…

I believe that 95% of all dogs are more loyal, honest and trustworthy than 95% of all humans. Those who dislike dogs should not be trusted. Those who abuse them deserve a fate that—well—lets just say it makes the worst torture of the Spanish Inquisition look like a picnic.

I believe Coke is better than Pepsi, although RC Cola goes better with ribs.

I believe love should be expressed infrequently, and given only to a cherished few. Throw the concept around easily and its currency becomes of little value.

I believe the hardest thing in the world is being yourself.

I believe fishing with live bait is preferable to artificial flies 'cause it's too hard to hold a beer when managing a fly rod.

I believe fire is cool.

I believe those who would try and change your nature have not yet come to understand their own. If a person wishes you to be something other than what you are, they are simply trying to fill a void in themselves. Your well being and happiness does not enter into it.

I believe friendship is the only honest emotion, for it is given freely and—if true—involves neither guilt, judgment, expectation, criticism or resentment. All dogs know this. Most people don't.

I believe people should learn to say no before they learn to say yes.

I believe a lot of stuff. Mostly I believe the best lived lives are those that don't let life get in the way of simple pleasures and tranquil peace. Don't take it too seriously. It's too short.

Yesterday morning there were 30 mule deer behind my house, the sun was warm. Later on I did a little work, scratched pup ears, looked at the patch of snow up in the mountain's big bowl, and had a drink with some friends.

Some folks are bored with days like that—not enough movement, too slow a pace—but I find them the ultimate celebration.

At age 40, the endurance of such things is the only gift I desire.

About the Author

The award winning editor, publisher and janitor of The Trout Wrapper magazine, Ron Marr's weekly column is syndicated in newspapers covering the northern Rockies.

Marr is also Pitmaster of The Pony Bar-B-Q, Pony, Montana. He can be reached via e-mail at http://www.ponybar.com

Photo Credit: Pamela Parsons

Printed in the United States
4098